The
Contemporary
Pastor

by Charles T. Crabtree

02-0461
Gospel Publishing House
Springfield, Missouri

ISBN 0-88243-313-X

Library of Congress Card Number: 00-105454

Table of Contents

1. The Call and the Election.....................................1
2. The First Days...11
3. Principles of Church Administration......................20
4. The Dynamics of Church Administration................. 31
5. Basic Philosophies of Church Administration............ 43
6. Church Administration:
      Office Routine...57
7. Church Finance:
      Philosophy and Routine Procedures....................68
8. Conducting Official Board Meetings......................81
9. Conducting the Annual Business Meeting.................90
10. The Art of Preaching......................................101
11. Observing Biblical Ordinances............................111
12. Conducting Weddings:
      Pre-marital Counseling and Preparations.............122
13. Conducting Weddings:
      The Wedding Rehearsal, the Ceremony,
      and the Reception.......................................131
14. Conducting Funerals.......................................147
15. The Role of a Minister's Wife............................157

Introduction

T his handbook differs in both content and style from others which have been written for ministers. My desire in writing this material is to give the new minister some shortcuts to a more effective ministry.

The reason for my informal approach is an attempt to come as close as possible to *being there* for the minister. This is a *hands-on* approach to ministry, beginning with the very first days of pastoring. Hopefully even the seasoned pastor will gain some added insights from this book which will further enrich his ministry.

There is a temptation to apologize for using a very personal approach to any kind of instruction. However, in this case there is a conscious attempt on my part to share personal experiences with the reader. There is also an attempt to *put words in the mouths* of young ministers.

The first chapter begins with the call to and election of the pastor. I have written this particular chapter primarily for the minister who has never pastored, but much of the material is also applicable to any minister who is facing the challenges of a pastoral change.

It is not my intention to give the impression that what I have written is the only or best way to do the things discussed in this manual. Through long experience I have learned there are always better ways if you keep your mind and heart open to the Spirit's leading. That is the lifelong challenge of the ministry.

Pastoral ministry is, at the same time, the most difficult and the most rewarding experience of a lifetime. It pulls everything out of you. The continual pressure to respond to different needs and situations is a constant challenge. For this reason alone it must be understood that no book, guide, nor manual will ever be able to cover all the contingencies of the pastor's job. It is my desire to simply make the task a little easier.

In every chapter I have only scratched the surface of the subject addressed. However, for those who have never pastored, this will perhaps give you a start. I am confident that the God who called you to pastoral ministry will take you far beyond the pages of this manual.

There are times I wish I could take what I have learned throughout the years and start again. But, in the wisdom of God, that is not possible. He gives every new generation of preachers their own opportunities for change and for ministering. It is a great comfort to know that there is a new army of God-called pastors who will take the experiences of the older ministers and do it better for their generation and to God's glory.

May the words that I share with you in the next few hours as you read this book be a blessing to your work. I pray these thoughts will help to make the load you bear just a little lighter.

Charles T. Crabtree

Chapter 1

The Call and the Election

C ongratulations! You have now received that *most important* telephone call. There is a possibility of candidacy for your first pastorate; you have been asked to meet with a church board! *What a thrill!*

However, you now face one small problem. You have never done this before. You are just a little frightened and have a multitude of questions you would like answered.

It is because of these things that I find it a delightful task to help you through this challenge--as well as others you will face down the road--making some of these experiences easier and your first pastorate a joy. We will first look at the call you have just received and the possible situations you will face through what is termed the *election process*.

Most of the time the call will come from the chairman of the pulpit committee at the church seeking a new pastor. He will ask if you are interested in considering a change of ministry, with the possibility of pastoring their church. The first principle you should learn and maintain throughout the entire procedure is to *BE DIPLOMATICALLY HONEST WITHOUT FEAR.*

If you are interested, you may say, "Yes, Brother Jones, my wife and I have been praying about a pastoral ministry and I am honored you have called me. I am very open to exploring the possibilities with you."

At this point, most boards have a proposed schedule in mind. Often they will ask for a resume. If you have a resume ready, a large part of your work for the next few days is already done. If you do not have a formal resume, simply tell them, "My wife and I do not have a formal resume, but I would be glad to send you a detailed letter in the next few days which will give you the pertinent information about our background. Would that be alright?"

In writing a letter of information or a resume, you should include:

1) the birth date and birthplace of both you and your wife.
2) your family background: your parents' names, their spiritual history and vocation, number of brothers and sisters.
3) your spiritual history: the date of your salvation and when you received the baptism in the Holy Spirit.
4) your church involvement prior to entering the ministry.
5) your formal education.
6) your experience in ministry and any other career information impacting your ministry.
7) your general condition of health.
8) your spiritual gifts and natural talents.

The letter or resume should be neatly typed and free from grammatical errors. It should be brief and to the point. This first correspondence with the church board is not intended to take the place of an interview. Mail your response quickly; don't worry about appearing too anxious. Boards today are usually impressed when they receive information quickly.

The Interview

Before the interview, find out if the committee wants your wife to be with you. If you must stay in town overnight, arrive early. Get settled in your room and spend time in prayer. Get your motives and your priorities straight! Go to the interview desiring God's will more than your own.

Dress as you would for a Sunday morning service. Most interviews are informal.

You should approach the interviewing board genuinely interested in each person present and in the needs of the church. This will allow you to get your mind off yourself and on the potential ministry opportunities with these men. While the interview is often informal, don't be too *chummy*. Show respect to each person. You are not in charge of the meeting so do not *take charge*--show respect as a guest.

Answer all questions candidly, without rambling. Be precise and to the point. Remember the first rule: *BE DIPLOMATICALLY HONEST WITHOUT FEAR*. You are being interviewed. These men are wanting information. They deserve honest and complete answers.

What Should You Ask at an Interview?

In order to gain proper perspective about the church, obtain information from those interviewing you. After the board has asked you their questions, ask the person chairing the meeting if he would mind if you ask some questions and make some comments. The chairman will, undoubtedly, give you this privilege. I suggest you seek the following information if you did not obtain it during their part of the interview.

1) Request an annual report, the Constitution and By-Laws of the local church, and a recent financial report to study.

2) Carefully go over what they expect of your wife and family. Give them the priorities of your life:

    a) your relationship with God.

    b) your relationship with your family.

    c) your ministry to the church. It is well to reassure the board members that your family will understand significant emergencies and will adjust for special circumstances.

3) If you have convictions in the following areas, this will be a good time to bring them out:

    a) your priorities in pastoring: i.e., pulpit ministry, counseling, visitation, involvement in community affairs, relationship to your denomination, etc.

    b) your expectations of board members in faithful attendance and financial support of the church.

    c) your desire to handle the business of the church in a business-like manner, with full disclosure to the members, etc.

4) I have never asked a board about money for myself. I have simply said, "I know you will provide adequately for my family. If the church grows under my ministry, I will assume my salary and benefits will grow accordingly."

You will be able to tell by the financial report what the pastor is paid. Bringing the subject of money up too early doesn't set well. There will be time for that. The board usually brings up the subject when they feel comfortable to do so. If the pastor's salary is disgracefully low, you may have serious doubts about going to the church; this fact could reveal a wrong attitude in many things.

I would also ask if moving expenses are provided. During this discussion, it would be good to clarify the length of time you would need between election and coming to the church. Thirty days is the normal time for this transition.

5) End the meeting by asking permission to pray. Claim God's perfect will for this situation. Remember to thank all board members for the privilege of being with them, and for their hospitality.

The Try Out

I never have liked the term *try out*, but it's about the only term we use to describe that eventful day or week we spend at a church with a view toward becoming the pastor--in the will of God. Candidacy sounds a bit political.

The principle of *BEING DIPLOMATICALLY HONEST WITHOUT FEAR* needs to be reinforced at this point. The following is a list of do's and don'ts which should be adhered to.

DO:

    * Go to the church honestly wanting God's will. A church may *look* right, but it may not *be* right for you. The goal is not to get a church, the goal is to find God's will!

    * Go to the church honestly desiring to minister to the people effectively on that day, showing love and compassion. Try to keep from being self-conscious. Lose yourself

in ministry to the people.

* Be your best self, but be yourself. If they won't like you at your best, they are not going to like the person you are trying to be, and they will soon discover the image you tried to project was phony.

* Your messages that day should be basically inspirational and uplifting--not so much instructive or corrective.

* You and your family should dress well without being ostentatious. Clean, neat, and pleasant are the practical orders of the day.

* Have a contact person (perhaps the chairman of the pulpit committee) who will handle all requests for food and fellowship. The board may have plans, or there might be a unique problem you don't know about. Simply say to all requests: *"We would be delighted, but do you mind checking with Brother _____ to see if he has made any plans for us?"* Many conflicts can be avoided by clearing your schedule through one person. Interest in you and your family will be at an all-time high.

* Thank the board publicly for their invitation and hospitality. Assure the people you will be praying with them for God's will in this decision.

DON'T:

* Set a lot of preconditions. I personally think many methods in choosing a pastor are inadequate, but you must work with what is acceptable and not try to change procedures at this point. If you have a real problem with the way the church handles the change of pastorates, graciously decline their offer, but don't try to change their procedures. If you can't handle the archaic method of trying out three or four preachers in one business meeting, simply say to the chairman of the committee: *I am not comfortable with letting my name stand with the others because it is confusing to the people.* Once you start the process, follow through with grace. There will be time to make a final decision. Too many men have missed God's will because they did not care for one part of a process which would have ultimately led to God's will.

   * Don't be crude, make ethnic jokes, tell jokes about mental illness, or tell stories which could be construed as off-color in any way. *THESE ARE STANDING ORDERS!*

   * Don't brag about what you have done or where you have been. When asked, be conservative in your answers.

   * Don't criticize your church Fellowship in any way.

If possible, request to meet with the board for a few minutes at the end of the day. Tell them if you feel led to let the congregation vote on you. If you know it is not right, tell them. If there is an overriding reason why you could not accept the pastorate, tell them. Congregations need to know if they are doing something which discourages good pastors from considering their church. Again, assure them of your continued prayer concerning God's will.

In some rare situations the church meeting takes place immediately. You have no choice but to let them go through the voting process unless you are absolutely certain you could not accept the pastorate. In that case, I would say to the people:

   "You have been most kind to me and my family. We will always remember you. We came seeking God's will. The Lord has made it clear that I have come to minister to you for this time in the will of God, but it is not His will for me to be your pastor at this time.

Instead of feeling discouraged or negative, I believe we should rejoice together because He has revealed His will. Let us pray together for God's will in leading you in your search for your new pastor."

The Election

Most elections will take place a few days after you preach. During that interim time, be constantly in prayer for God's perfect will. Ask the chairman of the board or the board secretary to call you as soon as possible after the business meeting--no matter which way the election goes.

Some ministers have strong convictions concerning the percentage of votes over the required amount to elect a pastor. If you don't get the required amount for election, it doesn't matter what your conviction is. If you don't get elected, don't fight it! Don't request another meeting.

I personally think any percentage over 80 is a good mandate. You should, of course, realize that a few people may be voting with ulterior motives--perhaps a desire to get a relative in as pastor or a desire to try out more candidates.

Have a basic acceptable percentage in mind so you can tell the church, through the person who calls, whether you accept or decline.

If you are elected and accept, request that an official letter from the secretary of the church be sent to you and to the district superintendent as soon as possible. This letter should contain the official vote and declaration of your election.

Upon receipt of the official letter, respond to the board with your own letter of acceptance. Send a copy of your acceptance letter to the district superintendent. This is very important for a clear flow of information.

Interim

I have always written a letter to be read to the congregation during the interim. I express my firm conviction of God's will, my love for my new congregation, and my enthusiasm about the future. Make them feel their new pastor wishes he could be with them immediately.

If the church provides a parsonage, your decision concerning where you will live is made. If you have a housing allowance (which is preferable in the long-term), you need help in finding the right housing. If you live a long way from your new pastorate, it would be wise to have a member of the board secure temporary housing so you will have time after assuming the pastorate to make an unhurried, wise decision concerning permanent housing.

It is wise to get recommendations about real estate agents, insurance salesmen, and professional services through your contact on the board. Don't make a commitment about such matters, even to a member of the church, without first checking with a responsible person in leadership. There may be serious ethical business problems you don't know about. There may be two or three insurance or real estate people in the church. Let official representatives of the church help you make these decisions.

Arrange with the chairman of the pulpit committee to set up your installation service with the district officiary. It is preferable to have all celebrations on welcoming day. It is, however, acceptable to have the installation service a few weeks after you arrive if it is impossible for the district officiary to arrange their schedules to be present on your first Sunday as pastor.

Make certain someone promotes the installation service with a good advertisement in the local paper. Most newspapers are glad to print a news release, free of charge, about a new pastor in their community. Don't let that opportunity slip by because of false modesty.

I have always preached a revival series the week following the installation Sunday. I begin the revival on Tuesday and have services each night--except for Saturday--through Sunday. This does many things. It allows your people to invite their friends to *hear the new pastor*, and it sets them on a good spiritual course. Often they have been so busy with the business of getting a new pastor, they have not had the chance to really enjoy times of worship.

This mini-revival also gives you an opportunity to minister and pray with your people, to begin learning their names. God has brought about some wonderful times of healing during these initial revivals. You just can't argue with a new pastor who wants to see revival in the church.

Preach Jesus. Preach faith. Believe God for new converts your first week.

If you go ahead with an introductory revival, have someone prepare advertisements and public relations materials early so the revival series can be promoted. In all probability, you won't be there to handle publicity, so the official board will have to work out details. Ask them to arrange special music for each service as well.

You have been elected! You are excited!

At this point, all I can say is:

WELCOME TO YOUR FIRST PASTORATE! YOU HAVE A REAL ADVENTURE AHEAD OF YOU!

Chapter 2

The First Days

Y ou are now into some of the most interesting and important days of your ministry. What you do and do not do will live with you for a long time. This chapter simply gives you a checklist of principles which will, to some degree, be valid for the rest of your ministry. These are especially important during your first days.

> *Principle #1: It is wise to avoid change as much as possible during your first few months as pastor.*

The change of having a new pastor is enough of an adjustment for the church to handle. Assure the people you are not going to make too many changes too quickly. Let them know you will keep the programs which are working well as long as they are viable. Where changes are obviously necessary, make the changes as gradual as possible, and always after careful deliberation and prayer.

Many ministers make changes based on what they have seen other churches do effectively. But you must remember that just as all individuals differ, your new church also is different from any other church. I have watched in shock as some pastors, within a few weeks following their elections, seek to "turn the church around" by making numerous basic changes. Pastoring is a work of patience. It takes time to earn the right to change the direction of a church.

I have often compared new pastors to heart transplants: *The initial surgery usually is successful, but the critical time is when some parts of the body have a tendency to reject the heart.* Your first few months as pastor should be looked upon as a time of restoration to the body. You are the heart of your church. Understand the need for the body to accept the heart as its own.

Another reason you should be extremely careful about making changes during your first few months is because you do not have enough data about the entire church operation and enough history about the church to know what will and what will not work effectively. When you find it necessary to make changes, allow for an option. If I were going to change something basic, such as a new service time or instituting an elective adult Sunday school curriculum, I would put it on a 6-month trial. Very few people argue with "let's give it a try" when they know they are not locked into the new concept if it is not successful.

How you handle change in your first days will undoubtedly have far-reaching consequences--consequences which will often affect your entire pastorate.

> *Principle #2: Don't be led into the luxury of criticizing your predecessor.*

This is one of the most subtle traps you can fall into. The principle of "If you can't say something good about a person, don't say anything" fits here beautifully.

You are the last person who should make negative comments about the former pastor and his family. Almost every criticism of a former pastor will be picked up by some who didn't like him. This tempts some ministers to fall into the trap of trying to make themselves look good at the expense of another.

When people in the church talk about their former pastor, they have already formed an opinion about him. What they are doing now is forming an opinion about you. That opinion will be much better if you have positive comments about the former pastor, or none at all.

If you uncover something illegal or immoral about the former pastor, the place to discuss it is with your district superintendent, not your new congregation. If the man has left behind problems the church must deal with, work through your board to take care of these situations. But again, do not single out and criticize the former pastor. Put all necessary criticism in a positive rather than a negative form of reference.

A statement to your board, such as "Brethren, I believe WE have a problem. Certain bills have not been paid and it appears there is not as much money in the treasury as we thought," is much better than attacking the former pastor.

If the problem is very serious, the former pastor may need to be disciplined--but not by you or your board. In the Assemblies of God, pastors are not disciplined by former church members, they are disciplined by the district officials.

When a criticism about the former pastor is made to you by a member of the congregation, do your best to ignore it. If a comment is necessary, say something like, "The former pastor had his strengths and weaknesses just as I do. But he did some good things for this church." Find the strong points of your predecessor and speak of those things. In the days to come, you may find that he acted in the only way he could under a given set of circumstances.

If the former pastor left in good standing and was generally loved, it would be very important to say to people who miss him, "Yes, your former pastor is a fine man. I want him to come back from time to time to visit and minister to us." You will gain great respect by speaking well of your predecessor. The love of the people for their former pastor reveals a capacity in the people to love you.

> *Principle #3: Accept as many invitations into the homes of your people as possible.*

You will be tempted to try to get your house and office in order at the expense of visiting with your congregation. You must realize, however, that the first days are vital in becoming acquainted with your people. You are in the people business. *Things can wait...people cannot!*

Throughout your time as pastor you will need to set up times to spend with your family. You should let people know you already have an appointment if they ask to see you during one of these preset family times. Appointments with your family are higher priorities than regular church appointments.

In the first couple of months, however, I would "strike while the iron is hot" and use the high interest in "wanting to get acquainted with the new pastor and his family" as an unparalleled opportunity to get acquainted with church members and families in their homes on a one-on-one basis. After that initial time, make certain you keep those times you have set aside to be with your family.

Your family should be instructed to be friendly and open when visiting the homes of your new congregation. They must never be critical. They should show interest in your host and hostess. You can make a game of seeing how much can be learned and remembered about each family you visit. Your investment in a relaxed social time with a family in your church will be rewarded time and time again.

When a family has gone to the trouble of preparing a meal and spending time with you and your family, you or your wife should immediately write a letter thanking them for their hospitality. Refer to the children of your host and hostess and mention a few pleasant occurrences of the evening.

Principle #4: Be sure to attend the first meetings of your ministerial fellowships on a denominational and/or city level.

I have found that cooperation and interest with your peers in ministry is a great privilege. Your church people will be relieved to know you are cooperative. After all, you will be asking them to cooperate with you. To cooperate with those in your community presents a good role model for all concerned.

Close to the beginning of your pastorate, invite your presbyter and his wife either to your home or for an informal lunch or cup of coffee in the city where he ministers. You need to quickly learn the dynamics of the section and become acquainted with what will be expected of you in the section. Participation in district and sectional functions is an important part of ministerial life. Ask your presbyter questions concerning how you can best fit in and how the district operates. Ask him to explain any other areas about the district and section you do not understand. He will welcome your interest.

Principle #5: During your first days, make it a secondary priority to meet as many people as possible in the business community.

It takes but a few minutes to make yourself known to the officers of the bank where your church has its account, the religious editor of the local newspaper, and to those suppliers and service people with whom you will be working as a pastor in that community. These acquaintances will prove invaluable as you minister.

In rural towns it is important to meet your church members and those in the business community as quickly as possible. Make certain you are well dressed and that your appearance is neat. During these relaxed days a suit and tie is not necessary for informal trips to town. However, your casual dress should be coordinated and your appearance considered. People will resent hearing that their pastor "sure looks sloppy and unkempt."

I have always made it a point to visit the administrators of the local hospitals as soon as possible. Learn the general routine at the hospital and become known by the receptionists and hospital chaplain. This will be invaluable in emergency situations.

Principle #6: You may have the unfortunate experience in your first days of learning that there are some power struggles and personality clashes in your new church. It is here you must adopt the principle of being wise as a serpent and as harmless as a dove.

Approach the problem with the attitude that you are going to pastor **all** the people. Let your people know you are not going to give preferential treatment to some in the congregation just because of who they are and what they have. The only exception to the non-preferential principle is when you are dealing with those who are sick.

No individual or group of individuals in the church should run the church. Never allow yourself to run the church for yourself or make decisions for selfish purposes. From the first day to the last day of your pastorate in that church, your members must possess a strong conviction that you will put the interests of the church above personal and/or special group interests when decisions are made.

In dealing with subtle attempts to manipulate you or attempts to discredit other members, I encourage you to ignore what is being said and refuse to "rise to the bait." Where there is no proof of the truth in accusations, there is nothing concrete. If you do not have something concrete, there may be a spiritual problem to watch for and pray about.

When it is an open challenge to get you to side with a particular person or group, you will have to be very frank and yet not be offensive. Respond by saying, "I'm sure you will learn that I am open to hearing all sides of an issue. I will do my best to consider all suggestions and proposals. I know you want me to be pastor to all in our congregation."

In the area of strained personal relationships, you must constantly seek the wisdom of the Lord. Some of the problems in a church have been there for years.

A new pastor is often tempted to become personally involved to show he is in control. Some problems are to be solved through spiritual growth. Carnal wisdom often compounds problems instead of solving them.

In some situations these attitudes are found among the church board members. I will be discussing the special relationships you will need to build and maintain with board members in a later chapter.

Principle #7:   The first days are to be days of gathering information without making decisions.

Before decisions can be made, make sure you learn what decisions really **need** to be made. You cannot do this without taking time to observe and listen to what is happening in your church and community.

Gather information about the community. Obtain written material concerning the history and future plans of the city. Take time to drive through the streets, becoming familiar with the area so you can respond to emergencies. This will also give you the knowledge needed to respond when people talk about areas in their community.

As you gather information, do so with a prayer for vision and resources to reach this community for Christ. Every farmer knows his harvest field and in what stage the harvest is at all times!

Gather information about your church. Learn its history. But more importantly, become familiar with the vision of your congregation. Listen carefully. Do not make comments or commitments too quickly. Carefully analyze the spiritual, physical, and fiscal trends and directions of the church.

Gather information about the departments in the church. Keep a notebook about each department's strengths and personnel. Have informal talks with department leaders. Become aware of their feelings. Learn where they feel their departments are presently. Learn about their visions for their areas. Early in your pastorate is not the time to make significant changes, but it is time to gather data and background and begin the process of considering changes.

Gather information about individuals in your congregation based upon your personal communication with the individuals themselves. Remember always that reputations are built on history, and that many times those reputations are derived from a single incident.

People should have the privilege of starting fresh with you, relating to you without having to rehash past failures. Quite often I have found that people who had a reputation of being hard to get along with are some of the most flexible and comfortable people I have ever known. Receive information about others, but make decisions based upon your own relationship with them.

Your first days should basically be enjoyed as a time to become a friend to your people. No matter how inadequate you feel at first, remember that you cannot fail if you genuinely love your new flock.

Be at the door of the church to greet them as often as possible. Try to remember names. Be relaxed.

Above all, *remember that God has called you to this church and He will help you meet the challenges and opportunities of your new church with a very positive attitude.*

Chapter 3

Principles of Church Administration

I t is hard for most new pastors to believe that 90 percent of church work is routine and repetitious. Because of this, many pastors have the tendency to spend years recreating the wheel. In other words, they are constantly rewriting the same correspondence, re-doing the same procedures, and re-learning the same lessons--over and over and over.

If you cannot believe church work is 90 percent routine, please believe that a high percentage of church work is repetitive. If you accept that one premise, it will get you thinking in the right direction to meet the challenge of church administration with some degree of skill.

Since much church work is repetitive, you can anticipate and prepare for most of the work ahead of you. This will allow more and more of your time to be spent in person-to-person ministry, creative thinking, and personal enrichment.

I ask you to consider principles of church administration under three easily definable categories: *ACTION, REACTION, and INTERACTION.* Please study and assimilate these principles before you begin your career as a pastor/administrator.

The Principle of Creative Action in Church Administration

I have deliberately chosen this category first because I believe creative development of an idea is the cutting edge of good administration. In order to follow through with creative thinking, the administrator needs a workable plan.

Why do you suppose the Four Spiritual Laws have proven to be such powerful tools? It is because they put the creative action of God (salvation) into a clear plan. They remove the question of what to do, and they give the hearer a clear choice. Granted, the Holy Spirit must work in the heart, but the simple plan removes the mental blocks of confusion so decisive action can be taken.

There it is! Good administration clears away questions and confusion so decisive action can be taken. When there is no plan, the administration is trying to figure out what could be done instead of deciding what should be done.

All good creative action in administration has several basic ingredients, whether they have been defined or not. These are:

1. an attainable goal;
2. a definition of dynamics;
3. a chart of implementation;
4. motivation; and
5. control of function.

The process is simple, yet for several months, and possibly even years, you should consciously go through these steps one by one. Eventually you will build a conditioned system in administration which you will follow without even thinking about the formal outline. You will also want to train associates and lay people to use this same process.

Keep several copies of the five steps on hand to fill in when you begin formulating a new idea. Don't cheat. Every step is necessary.

As an example, let's take a hypothetical project and follow it through this process. Let's take creative action toward your Sunday school. It is sluggish, boring, and stagnant. It has been running between 50 and 60 for many years. It's time to grow. But how? Never get up and say, "If everyone will bring one guest next Sunday, we would double our attendance in 1 week!" About the only thing you have done is to state an attainable goal; all other parts are missing. Creative planning and church growth take work. So, let's get to work!

First, *set an attainable goal.* Most people yawn when pastors state goals. Why? Because they have heard optimistic statements for years--statements without foundations! An attainable goal is a goal which links faith with works.

An attainable goal should contain the following: *the ultimate goal and an intermediate goal.*

The ultimate goal is what you want to accomplish in a year. The intermediate goal is what you can reach in a shorter, yet still defined period of time.

Your Sunday school is running 60; an attainable goal over a 1-year period is 120. That is your ultimate goal. Intermediate steps can first be set as quarterly goals, then perhaps as monthly goals.

To be realistic, we need to chart the "growth" months and the "tough" months. Depending on your situation, you will need to set higher goals for September through November and January through May than you do for vacation months.

Let us assume you are planning your new Sunday school year in January. I would plan to start this drive to double your attendance from Easter of that year to Easter of the next year. Don't state your plan to double your attendance until you have the plan set in every detail.

Your ultimate goal is to grow an average of 60 above the previous year. Your intermediate goals for the year might look something like this:

April	100	May	100	June	100
July	85	August	85	September	115
October	140	November	140	December	140
January	140	February	145	March	150

After looking at what needs to be done, you might decide your ultimate goal is not attainable in a practical sense. Thus, you decide to set your average at 100 instead of 120. Already the discipline of administration is making you face reality.

Chart your intermediate goals so that your faith is compatible with your works. In every planned project, whether in programs, staffing, or departments, you should carefully and prayerfully work on goals.

You are now ready to take step number 2: *A Definition of Dynamics.*

This step is seldom taken, yet it is the very heart of a proper plan of action. In this step, define the reasons why you need to reach the goal, and, more importantly, define why the goal has not been reached before! It is at this point the administrator steps back from personalities (including himself) and faces the truth with brutal honesty.

Here we are dealing with Sunday school, but we could be dealing with church finances, services, other departments, or special programs. Every administrative entity in the church must go through this honest and realistic appraisal if you are going to know and face the truth about the church you pastor.

Your Sunday school has been running 60 for years. Why hasn't it been running 120? List the reasons.

A good place to begin is with personnel. List the names of those presently involved in the Sunday school. This list should include everyone from the pastor to the class secretaries. Be honest about each person's effectiveness. Are they given the encouragement and support needed? If they are given help, are they capable to do the job?

As pastor, what is your role in the Sunday school? Are you needed? Are you effective?

Perhaps you will immediately be faced with some difficult problems. These problems don't go away, they simply perpetuate themselves. Grade past performances, present effectiveness, and future potential for each person.

After examining personnel, look at the program itself. Key questions should include: *What is the need, and is the need being met with excitement through this program? What is the Sunday school doing to be and to become an exciting and powerful force?*

Mentally go through the entire Sunday school program. Begin at the front door of the church. Imagine yourself coming to Sunday school for the first time. *Does the program provide adequate care and information for visitors?*

Do regular members feel good about being in Sunday school? What happens in each class when it opens? Is the preliminary time well thought out? What is the curriculum? Are the teachers effective?

When Sunday school is over, is there adequate follow-up? Is there a good record keeping system to help with follow-up? Do the teachers get the proper information so they can do their follow-up?

Next, look at the facilities. Ask yourself these questions: *How much room is there? Are the rooms neat and attractive? Would*

I want to go to Sunday school in these facilities? What are the options if there isn't room to grow in the present facilities? Facilities are tools. You need the best tools you can get to meet the challenge and get the job done.

It is at this point that I make my greatest decision: *What is the level of priority?* We are often premature in setting priorities. We need a good feel for what needs to be done. I have not mentioned finances yet because I believe the priority determines the budget. When you have a God-given conviction that your Sunday school (or other ministry) is a high priority, the resources will follow.

After determining priorities, you are now ready to move to the next step: *implementation.*

Start with the program you believe needs to be implemented. Again, begin at the front door. *What do those coming to Sunday school need?* I believe it is a sense of well-being for those who are regulars and a sense of direction for those who are new. Implement a *greeters* program. For this you need sharp, happy, knowledgeable people with the answers to whatever questions they may be asked.

What types and age levels of people do we hope to attract to our Sunday school? What kinds of classes are needed? Does the present teaching staff and subject material meet the needs? You may want to add two or three elective classes. You may have need for a newly-married class or a class for senior citizens. Find ways to initiate new, exciting class subjects.

Meet with teachers on a one-on-one basis and see if they know the program and are with the program. Maybe you have a boring teacher in a strategic class. Set up special elective classes, allowing this boring teacher to be one of the choices.

In implementing new and exciting programs, seek to be inoffensive. Allow people to maintain some traditional structure if you must, but make new and exciting options available to your people who want to change and develop.

Get more people involved by sharing time and building a team of workers in each class. This adds variety, brings discipline, and develops people.   Also, this serves as on-the-job teacher's training.

What do you need to implement as far as facilities are concerned? Do you need larger rooms or more rooms? Be open to innovative change. *Do you need to implement an* "operation decoration" *to fix up rooms?* Often a contest and awards for the sharpest rooms make this work a lot of fun.

What are you going to implement? With whom are you going to implement your idea? How are you going to implement it? And finally, when are you going to implement it? All of these questions should be answered on paper prior to presenting your idea.   Why?   Because these answers are necessary in order to make clear decisions and set forth directions.

When all of this has been accomplished, you are ready for step number four: *motivation.*

You are not ready to motivate until your plans are ready.   The best motivation is a clearly defined operation.   The death knell of good ideas is sounded when the person with the idea cannot answer questions concerning how he or she proposes to implement the idea.

At this point it is time to enlist your "partners in progress." Maybe the program only warrants one other person to start with; however, you need to enlist a small corps of people to enter into the refining process with you. Ideas on kick off, public relations, and central systems are all part of what this group deals with. Remember, good administration is working through people.

When you have a good, workable plan, ask a small committee of interested and involved people to join you. Share your vision and ask them to help formulate the program.

Begin to transfer vision and accept suggestions. Make people feel part of the process. They are going to work the plan after you have planned the work. Take their suggestions!

Make adjustments in the master plan. Give credit for good, innovative ideas.

If you have a Sunday school superintendent, he/she must be part of this small group.

After you have finalized the program to double your Sunday school in a year, it would be well to make a presentation to the board. I have found out, through many years of church work, that the board needs to be sold on all new programs. If the small group you work with is sold and if the board is sold, you can sell it to everyone.

After the board has approved the basic plan--not all the details, just the basic concept--and the budget impact, it is time to motivate everyone who is going to be involved in making the program work. Set a target date well in advance when you want your full Sunday school staff to meet. It is essential to have full participation.

Your attitude at the first meeting is to share the burden and conviction of your heart concerning the Sunday school. Explain the potential. Build their faith. Lay out the possibilities. Enlist their help. Because you have a well thought out plan, your people will become excited.

Allow each class teacher to set his/her own goals. Don't put an imposed number on them. I have found that after a good motivational talk, teachers and workers will set goals almost too high. It is wise, as part of the motivation, to let them set their goals at the end of the meeting and then total them. You will be amazed at how your faith will be translated into the minds and hearts of those you are motivating.

Ask for ideas on how to improve your proposed plan for

implementation.

Set another meeting date to finalize the campaign. The first meeting should convey the feeling you know what you want, but that you are honestly seeking input. After the first meeting you will be able to tell how excited people will be about the proposed plan.

Get back with your small committee. Make adjustments and get ready for the next meeting with the full Sunday school staff. This will be the meeting in which you will move to the details of the final step: *control of function.*

About 6 weeks before the initial thrust is presented to the entire church, you need to have every person and everything in place. Control of function is probably the most neglected and yet the most important part of church administration. It is this final meeting with your Sunday school staff which will give detailed instruction and control to your people. Have materials typed for every person.

A Sunday school promotional plan and control system should have the following data and instructions typed on a card:

Person's Name_____

Campaign Name and Theme_____

Dates_____

Overall Goal _____ Your Class Goal_____

Special instructions and information _____

Reporting Procedures_____

Special Arrangements for Promotion_____

Decoration of Classroom_____

Enlisting Help of Students_____

Prizes or Recognition for Involved Students_____

Date of Next Meeting_____

Throughout the entire campaign, meet with the staff on a regular basis to obtain reports, and to give recognition of achievement, motivation, special directions, and inspiration. Regular meetings and reporting keep the program on course. They will also help the staff to feel part of the team.

Though I have used a large effort (doubling your Sunday school attendance) as an example of how to create and follow through on a plan, I strongly recommend you take the five principles I have shared with you and try them on several smaller projects before attempting a large campaign.

For instance, let us use an example of creating a better church bulletin.

Your goal: to create the best possible bulletin without major expense.

Definition of Dynamics:
Why isn't it a good-looking bulletin?
1) Poor cover, bad printing, dull material, etc.
2) The impact should be sudden and positive.

Implementation:
1) Ask permission from the board to improve quality of stock.
2) Enlist help of good typist.
3) Write a new format with interesting details, etc.

Motivation:
Dependent upon myself and the response of the people.

Control:
Week by week assessment of each bulletin, not only

to maintain quality, but also to improve the publication.

Once you have started to grasp the basic ingredients of creative action through administrative guidelines, you will become excited about how easily you can take an idea from the realm of vision and turn it into a reality.

Chapter 4

The Dynamics of
Church Administration

According to the Scriptures, you are the earthly head of a living body of believers--a body which has both blessings and liabilities.

In this chapter I will deal with the dynamics of church administration in three major parts. All of these are a combination of tangible and intangibles. Church administration is not one or the other, but both.

The three parts are:

     I. The Dynamics of Tension
    II. The Dynamics of Balance
   III. The Dynamics of Productivity

Part I - The Dynamics of Tension

Many pastors never learn the inherent tension in church

administration. They spend their lives trying to avoid tension instead of using it.

The inherent tension is defined as the tension between "*Internal Control*" and "*External Change.*" In other words, you are living with a dynamic process which needs inward stability while, at the same time, also needing flexibility to respond to human need and inevitable change.

Your physical body has a miraculous inward control system which continually monitors and maintains the body. If your temperature begins to rise, all kinds of systems go to work to stabilize the internal temperature so the body will not be damaged. The circulatory and electrical systems of the body are all in place to keep and maintain a healthy body. With too much variance in these systems, the body becomes sick, often resulting in death.

The human body is subject to many types of external stimuli. The weather changes, the body adapts. The body is injured in an accident, the internal systems make automatic adjustments to restore the injured parts.

In the operations of a church, those who do not understand and use the tension between the need for strong administrative controls and the need to remain adaptable and flexible usually wind up taking one of two extreme forms of administrative styles.

One of these extremes is the administrator I like to call Mr. Machine. He does everything right, but runs over everybody in the process. Mr. Machine is one of those task-oriented people who believes the most important thing about a church is the machinery, not the ministry.

Mr. Machine has never learned that good administration is a servant and not a savior. The machinery of the church is not an end in itself, it is a glorious gift to the church to get the job done.

Richard Shelley Taylor, in his excellent book entitled "The

Disciplined Life" [Beacon Hill Press, Kansas City, MO, Pp. 46-47, 1962], gives real insight to those who tend to lean toward big machines instead of ministries:

"It is a mistake to suppose that disciplined living is entirely a matter of rigid rule, routine, and habit; or that its highest exhibition is in being able to determine a course of action for the day and then batter one's way through at any cost. Too many other people and legitimate demands are apt to get trampled upon by that kind of obstinacy. Such self-discipline is too akin to bull-headedness and self-will. It may be a symptom of basic selfishness.

This may shock some, since they have struggled so hard to bring some semblance of order into their lives and cultivate a healthy respect for the clock. They know that only in rigid regimentation of time and energy will they reach maximum accomplishment. Having achieved a measure of such control, they want above all to keep the reins in a tight group, and they expect the world to stand aside and allow them to drive their well-ordered chariot through undisturbed. When the world jostles in and slows the horses and rocks the chariot, they are apt to be petulant. To whip the horses right on, brushing aside the intrusions and riding over the obstacles, is in their view a mark of strength. But there is a higher kind of strength. It is the ability to adjust without being deflected, to pause without stopping all day.

Far more important than our hidebound little systems are people. Helping people should be the supreme objective of all our self-discipline. The trains that are built to carry people should not run them down."

I have seen administrators who "ran over" people to keep the machinery going, but soon there were no people riding the machinery. They had all been run over.

The second extreme is the administrator I like to call Mr. Chameleon. He is so relational he changes not only color, but procedures, policies, and precedents to please the person with whom he is dealing. His greatest fear is conflict. Because of this fear, he will risk war to keep from having a minor hand-to-hand skirmish.

Here is how Mr. Chameleon operates. He sets a rule and makes an announcement in church. "From now on, we will not make any more wedding announcements during the morning services. We will put them in the bulletin and announce them on Sunday nights."

For a few months he follows that procedure. Then a real firm person of influence in the church tells him he must make the upcoming wedding announcement. After all, this is going to be a big wedding and many of the children's workers do not get the bulletin, etc.

Mr.Chameleon is so intimidated by that person, the next Sunday morning he says, "I know we've had a policy not to announce weddings on Sunday morning, but this is a very special wedding and I think everybody will understand how important it is under these circumstances to make an exception."

Mr. Chameleon will spend most of his ministry pleasing a few people while frustrating everyone else. He has not learned that stress is not a bad thing in administration, but it is distress which must be avoided.

What have we learned by studying Mr. Machine and Mr. Chameleon? Simply that you must not allow the need for stable, internal controls to take away from the need for adjustments to ministry and vice versa.

How can we use this inherent tension and not be destroyed by it? After learning the dynamics of tension in church administration, it is necessary to move on to the second step.

The Dynamics of Balance in Church Administration

The dynamics of balance has three integral parts. Each part functions at all times, therefore, the three must be kept in balance. These three parts can be summed up in three words:

Action. Reaction. Interaction.

Proper balance of these three will allow you to make the dynamics of tension work for you, not against you.

People often ask which of these three parts is most important. My reply is always, "When you can tell me which leg on a three-legged stool is most important, then I will be glad to give you an answer."

Every good church administrator needs to learn how to take creative action. The Lord put you in charge of the flock. He expects you to be a leader.

I have dealt with how to create new programs in the previous chapter. My purpose for referring to it in this chapter is to show how it fits into your total philosophy of good administration to assure balance.

You have often heard the time-worn phrase: *A church cannot rise above its leadership.* That statement is so true it needs to be born again in your heart by the Holy Spirit.

If you look at the leaders of the church in the past, you will find men of vision. Men who were not afraid to take action when they had a word from heaven and were clear on what action to take.

Every good church administrator needs to learn how to react with poise. The word *reaction* is a bad word to some because too often it is not part of a formula for successful administration. It has often become a whole style, making the administrator a reactionary who does nothing else. He has created so many fires by not taking proper action and learning how to interact, that he does nothing until there is a threat.

While this form of administration is wrong, good reaction skills are just as necessary to good administration as knowing how to take creative action. I will give you several rules to follow in proper reaction skills which I have learned over my 25 plus years of ministry.

> 1. *Choose not to react angrily.* If you lose control, you are guilty of that to which you are reacting. Never get angry in front of your people and strike out. Righteous indignation grows out of God-given convictions when others are being hurt. The only time Jesus got angry was when others tried to keep people away from Him. Righteous indignation is really a controlled anger for the glory of God. Most anger grows out of a basic insecurity. The Bible bestows special commendation upon the person who rules his or her spirit. Choose to be bigger than the smallness which creates wrong reaction.

The late T.E. Gannon used to love to tell how, in his first pastorate, he decided to change a door at the back of the sanctuary. Some people were against it, but he went ahead and did it himself. He said that when he got the door moved, three families moved right out through it, never to return.

Do not make impersonal things personal. Learn that there are few things which are important enough to cause you to take a stand against your people.

> 2. *Do not get excited over possible exaggerations.* When people get excited about a situation which

touches them, they often exaggerate. Even the most wonderful, Spirit-filled, mature, and godly people invariably exaggerate when they are involved emotionally.

"Everyone is upset."
"You mean, everyone in the church?"
"Well no, but a lot of people."
"Would you please tell me how many and who?"
"Well, I don't know, but everybody is talking about it."

Most of the time, those statements are simply exaggerations! It would be rare indeed if *everyone* knew about the problem. It would be rarer still if everyone who did know about the problem cared about it one way or the other.

When you hear all-inclusive words like *everybody, a lot,* and *the whole church,* do not get overly excited. Most often these type of remarks are greatly exaggerated.

3. ***Take time to sort out all the facts.*** This is one of the hardest of all disciplines.

If there is a problem in the Sunday school, gather only those people involved and get the facts. Do not pour water over a person or group of persons who are not "burning up." Take time to talk, then react *with all the facts.* Do not take a position or make a comment until you are convinced there are no more surprises.

4. ***Try not to take criticism personally or react emotionally.*** If the criticism is true, accept it and learn from it.

Many preachers are embarrassed when they make an error. Often they compound it by trying to justify a wrong action. When you are criticized unfairly, try to react in the same way you would if you were giving advice from the pulpit. In other words, practice what you preach. *Turn the other cheek!*

The third skill in administration is *interaction.* This is the art of working with a group of people and getting the job done through them.

Though you may be able to do things better and more quickly by yourself, unless you have the patience to learn how to work through people effectively, you will never become an effective administrator.

The art of learning how to interact leads to our third part of the dynamics of administration:

The Dynamics of Productivity

This section is actually the third part of the dynamics of balance, but it is so misunderstood, I have chosen to deal with it in a separate section.

The dynamics of productivity in administration are best understood by the following equation:

Expectation + Performance = Desired Output

This concept was clarified for me by a former staff member, Everett Bartholf, to whom I am indebted.

When you interact with people on a regular basis, two factors are constantly at play. First, you are performing your task according to what you perceive is expected of you--to fulfill your duty to the best of your ability. On the other hand, when you assign a task to an individual or to a group of people to perform, you expect them to perform the task a certain way. If you are not clear about your expectations, they will perform according to their expectations, not yours.

The reason ministers get in trouble in the area of administration is simple. They do not understand the need to line up everyone's expectations. This results in everyone performing their work in conflict.

We see this happening in every area of life. In marriage, the husband and wife must learn how to communicate this balance between performance and expectation. A good wife or a good husband is determined by his/her performance when viewed by the spouse's expectations. The same type of thing happens between pastor and people.

Pastor Present comes to the church. He is excited. He assures the people he is going to work (perform?) hard to make the church grow. He is sincere, but he works according to what he thinks (expects?) a pastor should do. His expectations of a pastor, however, differ from what the people expect from a pastor.

Their dear Pastor Former was such a good pastor. How did they know he was a good pastor? By how he performed in the role of a pastor. He visited in the homes of his members every month or so. He stopped by to help his people, and would take some of the older folks to do their shopping. He was not a great preacher, but he was a wonderful pastor.

Pastor Present wants to be a wonderful pastor, but his ideas and expectations of a good pastor differ drastically from Pastor Former. Pastor Present believes he should study hard; he longs to feed his people. In order for the church to grow, Pastor Present believes he must visit new people. He also knows he should spend time with his young family at least one full day, as well as a couple of evenings each week. Pastor Present is a hard worker, (even harder than Pastor Former) but he does not perform the way the people expect a "good" pastor to perform.

So the congregation compares Pastor Present with Pastor Former. Because he does not visit as a "good" pastor is expected to visit, because he is not buddy-buddy the way a "good" pastor should be, the people do not think their new pastor is much of a pastor. Both the new pastor and his people become frustrated.

It is easy to see what needs to be done. The new pastor should be very clear regarding what he believes a good pastor should do. He should carefully go over and over what makes a good pastor and how he will have to perform to meet his expectations.

He will have to share his priorities as a preacher/teacher. He will have to say, "I would like nothing better than to be able to visit all of you regularly, but the Lord has impressed me with the need to study long hours and to spend time with new converts in discipling them. I am sure the mature Christians in our church will immediately understand the need to set priorities. Other ministers have been very effective in setting their own priorities in how they pastor, but I must be faithful to the priorities I have set for my own ministry."

Nearly every year I have a *Person-to-Person* chat to answer questions about my ministry in the church. During this session, I share the expectations I have for my own life and ministry, and give the rationale as to why I perform my duties the way I do. When people understand your expectations, they can easily understand why you perform the way you do.

A minister called me sometime ago to share with me his frustrations with his youth pastor. He said, "For ten cents I'd fire him on the spot!"

When I asked why, the pastor replied, "He's lazy. I can't seem to ever find him. He's out of the office every afternoon."

"Do you know where he is?" I asked.

The pastor said, "Only God knows that!"

I replied, "I know God knows, but you should know!"

Then I added, "A lot of young men are taught in Bible school to spend time with their kids. Make sure he has a chance to explain what he is doing. I would not want a youth minister who was in the office all the time. I would expect him to spend a lot of time out with the youth in his group, as well as out meeting new kids."

Later the pastor called, a bit chagrined. His youth pastor had indeed been spending every afternoon with the young people of the church and the town.

This pastor had fallen into a trap of not telling the young man what he expected from a youth pastor; therefore, the youth pastor could not perform according to the senior pastor's expectations.

The youth pastor, on the other hand, should have been clear in explaining to the pastor where he was and what he was doing. These men did not educate each other's expectations.

Whenever you must work through a person or a group, be sure to discuss the job or task description so what you expect done is clear. Then, you must clearly describe your expectations so all involved will know how you want them to perform. Only when you take time to do this will you experience the kind of output you desire through administration.

The following two diagrams show the proper and improper flow of our equation:

Performance + Expectation = Desired Output

Right

1	2	3
PASTOR GIVES WORKER AN ASSIGNMENT	PASTOR GIVES WORKER GOOD JOB DESCRIPTION AND SHARES HIS EXPECTATIONS	WORKER PERFORMS WITH EDUCATED EXPECTATION

Result: two happy people. Worker is happy because he knows what is expected of him while he is doing the job. Pastor is happy because he has desired output from worker.

Wrong

1	2	3
PASTOR GIVES WORKER AN ASSIGNMENT	WORKER GIVEN NO JOB DESCRIPTION OR EXPECTATIONS	WORKER PERFORMS WITHOUT KNOWING WHAT PASTOR EXPECTS

Result: two unhappy people. The pastor is unhappy because the worker did not do the job as expected. The worker is unhappy because he "did his best" and did not please the pastor. His complaint: "Nobody told me what to do, so I did what I thought the pastor wanted me to do."

Chapter 5

Basic Philosophies
of Church Administration

From the smallest church to the largest you have an obligation to your people to develop them for the work of the ministry. Learning to work through people is often discouraging. However, you must either become skilled in this area or be stymied by the strength and size of your church.

After your church reaches 200 or 300 in attendance, the shift to administration becomes more and more significant. Remember, you need to learn the principles of administration while your church is very small if you plan to grow numerically and develop leaders among your people. Even a very small church has a great deal of activity which needs good administration.

Good administration is nothing more than giving people an opportunity to achieve within clearly defined guidelines so others are not adversely affected by their activity.

Good administration will help a church of any size because it releases people to do their jobs with faith, knowing they are making a significant contribution to the kingdom of God.

Throughout this manual I will use several words which may need clarification. The word *structure* will be used to describe any part of church work delegated to others which is routine in nature.

Systems are the tracks put in place for people and programs to run upon.

The word *control* is another word for accountability to authority. It is like installing traffic lights to avoid collisions. Controls will move the flow of church work through intersections. Through these controls you will know when work has been done or at what stage the work is at any given time.

Buy a large loose-leaf notebook and title it **Church Administration Notebook**. Divide the book into sections.

The first section should be entitled, "*How Things Are Done.*" This section will have three major sub-sections: "*Personnel,*" "*Programs,*" and "*Policies and Procedures.*"

The second section should be entitled, "*What Needs to Be Done.*" This section will also have three sub-sections: "*What to Keep and Strengthen,*" "*What Needs to Change,*" and "*What Needs to Be Added.*"

How Things are Done

You are now ready to begin the first step in church administration: gathering valid data.

Don't make decisions without knowing the facts. Your first sub-section under the section "*How Things Are Done*" is entitled "*Personnel.*" Since you're going to work through people, people should be your first consideration. List all personnel in places of leadership and the length of their commitment. On your first sheet under Personnel, list all board members. Find pertinent information about them through personal communication or information received from others.

Data on board members should include names of family members, their jobs on the board, if any, (such as officers, etc.), special abilities, when their terms end, and other pertinent information. After each annual business meeting, put your church's new slate of deacons at the front of your minute book.

Next, list your Sunday school staff. Begin with the Sunday school superintendent. List his/her family members, the term of office, etc. Then list the department heads, teachers, secretaries, and all other personnel. You may want to divide your personnel into ministry categories; i.e., children, youth, women, men, music, etc.

All personnel in areas of responsibility should be identified. This document will eventually be formalized and constantly updated. Your first order of business is to determine who you have to work with. All are assistant pastors.

Your next section is entitled "*Programs.*" In order to administrate well, be aware of and anticipate all activities which function on a regular basis. If you are not careful, you will find out too late that a traditional function or program of the church is part of your responsibility. Many people in your church believe the moment you become their pastor you automatically know everything about their church. After all, you are the pastor, aren't you?! As administrator take nothing for granted!

You can obtain most program information in a few hours by asking a couple of key leaders in the church to sit down and go over a church calendar with you. Remember, at this point you are still gathering information and trying to learn what is already functioning. Change comes later.

Divide your "Programs" sub-section into three categories:

weekly, monthly, and annually. Ask the people you meet with to help list all the weekly programs now functioning. This would include all age levels, from infants through senior citizens.

Often a new pastor is not aware of children and youth programs. Find out if the Royal Rangers and Missionettes meet weekly, where they meet, and how many attend on an average. Are there any home Bible study meetings? When and where are choir rehearsals? List every weekly activity you are personally involved in, including Sunday school, midweek services, etc.

List all monthly programs. In most churches there are monthly activities in every department. Do the men have a monthly meeting? Women's Ministries? You will be surprised how many things go on in even the smallest church on a regular basis. Water baptisms and Communion services should be included.

One of the most difficult areas to determine is annual events. It is wise to find a year-old calendar and make notations on what took place. List traditional activities and special days. Determine what role the pastor played in these events.

Ask such questions as: *Does the church have a traditional Good Friday service? Is a service held at Thanksgiving? What is done for programs at Christmas? Are there traditional picnics, pot-luck dinners, and church outings?*

It is also important to have a district calendar of events, listing those areas where your church cooperates and where you are going to participate personally. Include such events as youth conventions, district councils, general councils, and sectional activities.

For your **Church Administration Notebook,** enter as much detail under each event as possible, especially noting and highlighting what is expected of you as pastor.

When you have completed this section, get a large calendar and fill in every activity on a weekly, monthly, and annual basis.

Leave room on the calendar for additions. I would suggest using a pencil so adjustments can be made easily.

Post the events calendar in your office or the church office. Establish this as your master calendar of events. Begin to train the leaders of the church to get all activities on the master calendar. Emphasize that activities already posted on the master calendar have precedence over requests and plans for new programs.

Establishing and maintaining a master calendar is at the very heart of your systems and controls. Learn to update your master calendar at least once a week. You will eventually refer to it daily. It is good to keep a portable appointment calendar with you at all times, but be sure to maintain the large, master church calendar.

Your next section is entitled "*Policies and Procedures.*" As your church grows, this section will enlarge to a manual of some size. Many times procedures have been followed for so long they are actually unwritten policies.

The Constitution is your first policy statement. The By-Laws are a clarification of the Constitution, giving further detail. All policies and procedures are nothing more than further clarification and detail of your Constitution and By-Laws. Thus, outlining policies and procedures is nothing more than clarifying your chain of authority.

Carefully study the constitutional policies. Then, study the By-Laws policies. Underline and list in your **Church Administration Notebook** the By-Laws directives which affect the day-to-day operation of the church.

List official board policies. This takes some time and effort, but it is worth it. If I were you, I would go back 3 or 4 years in the Minutes of the Official Board and list policies that have been established. Policies are directives which are basically open-ended. In your notebook, create a sheet in the following manner:

Official Board Policies:

SUBJECT	DETAIL	DATE PASSED
Fund raising:	The board shall approve all requests for fund-raisers in all departments.	3/10/78
Medical ins.:	The church will pay all health insurance premiums for the pastor and his wife, plus half the premiums for his children.	10/2/78
Missions:	It shall be the policy not to allow individual missionaries to raise personal pledges by passing out pledge forms to the people. The board shall determine the monthly support of missionaries.	12/2/78

Most binding policies are through official board action, and should be listed as noted above. However, there are procedures you need to observe and note. Create another sheet in the following manner:

Departmental and General Procedures:

DEPARTMENT	SUBJECT	DETAIL
Public Relations	Newspaper ads	I do weekly ads, but Sister Atkins is artistic and draws up special ads.
Christian Education	Christmas gift to Sunday school superintendent.	The pastor has always arranged to present a gift to the

superintendent the Sunday prior
to Christmas. This gift is given
during the morning worship.

This section of your notebook will be invaluable throughout
your entire pastorate at the church. Keep it current.

The next section of your **Church Administration Notebook**
is really the challenge of the pastor: *What Needs to Be Done.*

As stated before, this area of your notebook should be divided
into three sub-sections entitled, "*What to Keep and Strengthen,*"
"*What Needs to Change,*" and "*What Needs to Be Added.*"

From the very first day you will see things which obviously fit
clearly into one of these three categories. The area of change is,
at the same time, both exciting and risky. How and when you
make changes is as important as the changes themselves. This
is why you need to outline your goals very carefully and plan your
procedures in detail.

Your first sub-section is "*What to Keep and Strengthen.*"
Throughout your entire ministry you should maintain the philosophy that no one is excited by excellent but sloppy preparation. Also remember that unnecessary ignorance can offend
many, sometimes to the point they will never return to church.

Obviously you will want to keep personnel, programs, and
policies which are working well or *will* work well with a little
guidance. You will also undoubtedly want to build upon the
people already in place. We will deal with difficult people in the
next few paragraphs.

You will want to keep and strengthen basic programs, such as
the Sunday and midweek services, Sunday school, children's
programs, youth programs, and adult programs, etc. The
purpose of your administration will be to strengthen and build
upon good solid programs.

Keep in focus those areas which run unusually well. Behind these well-run programs are good people who may prove to be keys to your more ambitious and progressive plans later.

Your second section is entitled "*What Needs to Change.*" Almost immediately you will probably pick up on personnel who are disasters in certain areas. Be very patient. People will understand your patience, but they will resent it if you become impatient--even if they know you're right.

Take note of the personnel who must be eventually redirected or, in some cases informally retrained. In other situations you may find personnel who will have to be retired. Remember, the "how" and "when" is as important as the "what."

You will soon learn there are programs which need to be changed. Under this section, begin to list ideas and suggestions which will help in the overall program. Often pastors have wonderful ideas, but simply tack them on to a bad system. Then they wonder why their ideas didn't work.

Watch, listen, and ask questions for a period of time until you not only learn the ingredients of a church program, but also learn why the chemistry or mixture does or does not blend. Good changes take time, insight, and patience. For instance, if changes are needed in the music department, begin to examine new people and ideas which would better the program. The same is true when reviewing the worship services and other areas of your church.

Remember to strive for excellence. Don't exchange a mediocre program for another mediocre program. Get ready to exchange a mediocre program for an excellent program.

List all the things you see which need to be changed--from the church sign, building, or bulletin, to all other areas. Determine how and when you will make recommended changes.

In obvious areas you could suggest some non-personnel changes soon after you arrive, especially if the resources are available. Suppose the old church sign is a disgrace. Since the name of a new pastor needs to be added, it would be in the realm of common sense to suggest to the board they consider a new sign immediately. It is reasonable and important to project a better image to the community.

Many little things can be changed without threatening anyone. I used to go to the church every Saturday night for prayer. After prayer, I would look over the sanctuary carefully. I would straighten all the hymnbooks, making sure everything was neat as well as clean. I got others to help me work outside the building, and we were able to make a startling difference at no cost. These are all improvements on what is already in place. If you are wanting to change something, such as a door or painting a room, you need to clear it at your official board meetings.

Your third section is entitled "*What Needs to Be Added*." I have already emphasized the need to resist the temptation to immediately make changes. However, there is nothing wrong with beginning to consider and clarify in your own mind what personnel, programs, and policies need to be added. As you ask questions and gather material, you will discover many gaps in your church organization which will need to be filled to provide good systems and controls for new programs.

In chapter 3 I have outlined how to effectively take a new program through from inception to completion. For the final section in your **Church Administration Notebook**, create the following pages: *New personnel needed. New programs needed. New policies and procedures needed.*

After you take the time to put your **Church Administration Notebook** together, you will not only have a working knowledge of the church in a very short amount of time, but will also be able to take your proper role as leader because you will know the facts about the organization.

Through the years I have observed that pastors who choose to discipline themselves to be good administrators not only are prepared for growth, but actually create the dynamics of growth.

In my opinion the single most neglected factor in church work is church administration. I believe this leads to the single greatest reason for loss of souls, lack of growth, and counterproductive activity.

You are now ready to put together your first administration flowchart. I say the first because as your church grows and adds activities you will have to enlarge your flowchart to include all new systems and controls.

The creation of a flowchart is obvious. It is the definition of what is happening under what authority. The flowchart forces you to be objective and factual about all areas of your church. A good church administrator will build a strong church body through a clear understanding of the anatomy of a church body. The flowchart is the skeletal structure of your church. Most pastors have problems understanding how a church should work because they have never taken the time to build an organization through which church life should flow.

In the spiritual flow of authority I view the top church authority like this:

Jesus. Pastor. Deacons. The flock.

As the pastor of the church, I feel I have been given spiritual authority over the board and members. That is why, from the very beginning, I insist upon the biblical right to preach what I want (being subject to the Word of God). I have also insisted on having the right to pick and choose who ministers from my church pulpit. In spiritual matters you are given great authority. The pastor should be careful not to lord it over God's heritage, but at the same time the pastor must not default on his leadership responsibilities. The pastor should never feel above his people as a person, but he must accept the authority of his role.

If you fully understand your spiritual role as the pastor, then you will not be threatened by your administrative role. I believe the dual role of spiritual leader and church administrator is a great check and balance on top leadership. In spiritual matters I am answerable to God. In administrative matters I am answerable to men. This balance keeps me free in the Spirit and at the same time accountable in the flesh.

Some pastors never accept for themselves or train their boards on this dual role. They are forever trying to operate by one or the other authority when they should use both. If you use only one authority structure for both pastor and administrator you will be frustrated.

For instance, I have seen pastors who used the spiritual authority structure to run the administration come to the conclusion that they are not accountable to a board or anybody else. Other pastors have used the administrative authority structure to operate the spiritual life of the church, resulting in a lack of boldness in the pulpit and fearing man.

In our chapters on church administration we will be using the flowchart for administrative authority. This is the legal authority to do church business. The pastor, as the administrator, is answerable to men.

I suggest a simple organizational flowchart for a small and/or moderate size church. Use this chart only as a guide, not as a rule. The body is a living, growing thing and should never be limited or in bondage to a structure which restrains, but should use structure to expand. However, the body should always be well defined to be functional.

The minute you start pastoring, you pastor two churches, not one! You pastor both the church that exists and also the church you see by faith. Faith is a new kind of seeing.

Here is the structure I would recommend for churches running
from 25 to 80 in attendance.

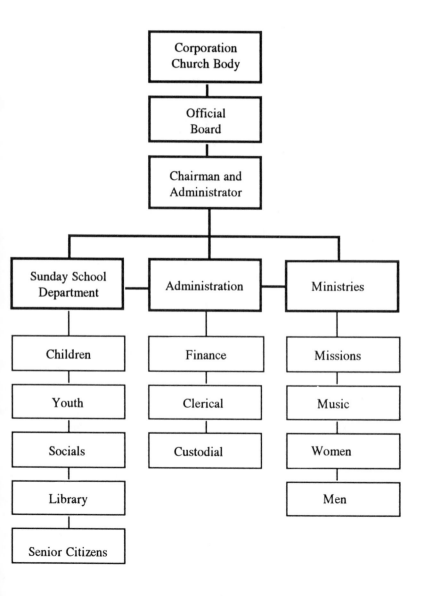

Be flexible about where you place all these areas of church work, but be specific. Perhaps you want other ministries under Sunday school or vice versa, but identify each area and place each under one of the three categories.

I recommend the following chart for churches running from 80 to 300 in attendance.

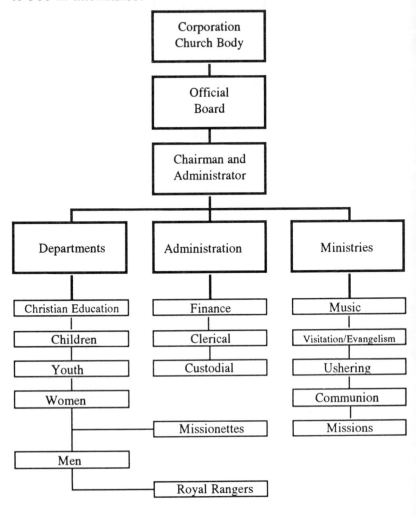

Refine this flowchart as you grow.   Add every significant ministry to your flowchart.   These are your structures.

Keep a small copy of your flowchart in front of your **Church Administration Notebook**.

Chapter 6

Church Administration: Office Routine

In your first church you are often the only person available to run the office. This is not a "negative," for a short period of time, because it forces you to become acquainted with all details of the church.

In order to give you a practical guide, I will take you through a week as office manager.

I am assuming you will choose to take Monday off. I prefer Tuesdays off, because Mondays are often filled with visitation, detail, and reflection from the previous day. However, when I pastored a small church, I took Mondays off.

In a church where I had to do everything in the office, I would plan to keep office hours from 1 p.m. to 5 p.m., Tuesday through Friday. During these hours I would discipline myself to be in the office, and I would tell my congregation that they could reach me at the church during those hours.

You will undoubtedly spend most mornings in the office as

well, but those morning hours are for handling the clerical work--answering phones, setting up appointments, answering mail, doing bulletins, etc. These morning office hours are in addition to those spent taking care of pastoral duties. Post your office hours and then keep them. If you must be gone during those times, have someone cover for you.

From the very beginning of your ministry, learn to conduct church business in a businesslike fashion. The need for set office hours gives your people and the community an image of efficiency and excellence. If you are going to be out of town, or if a conflict arises, have two or three people you can call upon to be in the office to answer the telephone and do other tasks you assign.

On Tuesday through Friday, take your lunch early so you can open the church office promptly at 1 o'clock. Your church office may only consist of a small room, a telephone, and a desk, but it is an important beginning to your work as an administrator.

Organizing Your Church Office

You will be amazed how much time you will save by taking a few hours to get ready for business.

In addition to a desk, chair, and telephone, you will need a typewriter. If you do not know how to type, you will have to beg, plead, or borrow a volunteer to do typing for you.

If your church cannot afford to purchase a typewriter, you will find that many larger churches will respond to a plea for financial help to purchase one.

You will also need office supplies. The minimum list of necessary supplies needed to set up an office are listed on the next page. You will note that I have separated these needs into two categories: *Supplies and Equipment.*

Office Supplies and Equipment

Supplies

1. Non-profit stamp
2. Tape/Tape Dispenser
3. Pencils
4. Pens
5. Exacto Knife
6. Exacto Knife Blades
7. Ruler
8. Rubber Bands
9. Paper Clips/Holder
10. Stapler/Staples
11. Staple Remover
12. Letter Opener
13. Eraser (Soft)
14. Scissors
15. Dictionary
16. Paper
17. Stationery
18. Envelopes
19. Binders (3-ring)
20. Rolodex File
21. Rolodex Cards
22. Writing Pads
23. Scratch Pads
24. Telephone Message Pads
25. In/Out Basket
26. Clock
27. Pencil Sharpener
28. Telephone Books
29. File Folders
30. Folder Labels
31. Church Mailing Labels
32. Wastebasket
33. Three-hole Punch
34. A/G Directories
35. Book Shelves
36. Tissues
37. Desk Calendar
38. Church Planning Calendar
39. Membership Card File
40. Membership Cards

Equipment

1. Typewriter
2. Computer/Printer
3. Adding Machine (or access to one)
4. Postage Machine (or access to one)

5. Copier
6. Five-drawer File Cabinet with lock
7. Desk/Chair
8. Telephone

Running a Church Office

From the beginning you will have to be diplomatic but firm about people coming to the church office to visit by the hour. You will have to start training people by telling those individuals who are obviously making a habit of being in the office all the time that, "As long as we can't afford an office secretary, I will be running the office. I would like nothing better than to visit during office hours, but please understand I will have to visit with you on my own time."

If you answer the phone and proceed with your work, they will soon get the message that it's not a good time to "chew the rag" with the pastor. When people seem to insist on remaining, I have asked them to pitch in and help me with the work.

Throughout your entire ministry you will have to learn how to handle well-intentioned but time-consuming people without offending them. Don't be too hard-nosed. People in a small church resent a pastor who seems unavailable.

Your first duty in any office is to take care of the mail. Keep your personal correspondence separate from mail addressed to the church. You will need to build a file for church business and correspondence. Discipline yourself in keeping all business for the church in the church office.

Keep your personal business in your pastoral office or study. Soon you will be turning the office over to a secretary and she will need things pertaining to the business of the church, and all of the correspondence to the church, in the church office.

Handling correspondence is important. Process the mail each day you are in the office. Do it first because correspondence has a tendency to pile up and get lost.

Set up a freestanding divider for sorting mail which goes to others in the church. Put the names of departments and/or individuals on the dividers. Place all information or business mail in the department or individual's divider that he/she will need to read and/or respond to.

For instance, your treasurer will need to have a place where he can pick up bills to be paid, as well as other information which he needs to do a good job. Department heads receive information from the denomination on a regular basis. Teach these people to stop by the church office on a weekly basis to pick up pertinent information that has been placed in their mail dividers.

After you have read all mail, immediately answer necessary correspondence. Promptness in correspondence is essential. If you do not have someone who types your visitor letters, do those and get your outgoing mail ready for mailing. If for some reason you cannot do the work right then, put it all in your action file--either a desk tray or a folder on top of your desk.

Make copies of all personal letters (except visitor letters) and file them in your correspondence file drawer. Alphabetical files are good for filing correspondence.

Church stationery should be the best you can afford, and should be professionally designed and printed.

Now you are ready to turn to your business diary. This can be an informal, loose-leaf notebook, or it can be an executive daytimer. Your church office diary is where you keep track of the order for the day.

On the first day of the office week, carefully list all the things needed to be done and place them in time slots in your church diary. Each event on the church calendar usually affects the church office in some way; i.e., public relations, room setup, and contacting people. Every event affects things and people. Good administration is learning how to anticipate details to avoid conflict.

Now go back to those things listed in the church diary that need to be done that day. In a short period of time you will establish an office routine which will, in turn, make it easy to teach and train a secretary when the church can afford to hire one.

Your Church Bulletin

Most pastors who are just starting out have the responsibility of putting together the church bulletin. Keep one thing in mind: a poorly done church bulletin is worse than none at all. In other words, if you choose not to do a neat job on a bulletin, don't put one out. There should be no misspelling. Always use good grammar. There shouldn't be any typing errors. Information should be placed in neat columns. Remember these do's and don'ts. They are all important.

A church of any size can afford to put out a good bulletin. To do so requires three things:

1) *Good Material.* Write material which is vital and interesting to your people. Put in all activities for the coming week. Alert people to events you plan to promote in the next quarter. Place brief news about the missionaries your church supports. Put in material you would find interesting and informative yourself.

2) *Good Layout.* If you are not good at layout work, get a volunteer to help you with this task each week after you have written the material. For pennies a week you can

subscribe to bulletin insert companies which provide all kinds of illustrative materials.

3) *Good Printing.* In all printing needs for your church you should strive for excellence. However, in no other area is good printing more necessary than for the bulletin. It is the first communication visitors receive from your church. The bulletin also tells people how much you care. If you cannot afford a machine which duplicates well, ask around until you find an office manager who will let you use a machine once a week for a few minutes. Whatever you need to do to produce a well-written, well-designed, well-printed bulletin, by all means do it!

Mailing List and Rolodex File

Your mailing list is the lifeblood of your church because it is necessary to communicate with your congregation from time to time by mail. It is important to build and maintain the largest, immediate-area mailing list you can.

I recommend you place every "*in area*" visitor on your mailing list. These visitors are your best prospects. If they do not want to be on your mailing list, they will either call you or refuse the mail.

There are many reasonably-priced methods which can be used to maintain the list and produce labels for mailing. For a list under 250 names, I recommend the perforated label sheets available at all stationery stores. You simply mimeograph a 3-month supply. Names can be easily added or marked out if people move or desire to be deleted from your mailing list.

Request an *address correction* on all publications and correspondence. The post office will return the mail to you at a small cost, but it is well worth it. Using address corrections will keep your mailing list current.

When sending 200 pieces of mail at a time, you can apply for a third class, non-profit mailing permit. This permit allows you to send out large mailings at a reduced cost. When my mailing list was around 150, I mailed 5 pieces to each member of 10 or 12 families so I could qualify for a bulk mailing permit. This saved the church a lot of money in postage costs.

Keep a master mailing list. Also, keep a copy of this list in your desk in your study at home. From the master list, keep the rolodex file in the church office updated.

On the rolodex cards, include the names of every member of the family. Note whether the family members are members of the church. Birthdays are also good to have on the cards if the information is available. Put work numbers (W) under home numbers (H) on each card.

As changes occur in families, make sure your files are changed. *Be careful to make these changes on all files you maintain.*

From the master mailing list you need to make special lists for Sunday school workers, youth workers, board members, and all others involved with different ministries in the church. With these lists you can readily send out notices to people without constantly having to do research to compile names and addresses.

Filing

Most pastors do not like the job of filing, but it is necessary for record keeping and ready referral. You will find all copies of first class mail invaluable. I cannot recount the times I have had to go to the files and pull information. With church business it becomes a legal protection.

For correspondence with individuals, your files become a personal protection. Your personal correspondence files should be kept in the church office because most of your correspondence will impact the church. Of course, letters to your immediate family members would be kept in your personal files.

Filing is basically an exercise in common sense. As areas of interest and correspondence multiply so will your files. Simply label file folders and discipline yourself to place all materials worth keeping into logical categories so you or anyone else can find the information quickly. With a volunteer file clerk or secretary, you will be able to set up your filing system in one afternoon.

Once a year you need to go through the files and discard obsolete and dated material.

When your church is financially able to hire a full-time or part-time secretary, there are definite qualities this person should possess. I have made a list of questions you must ask yourself before hiring a secretary. Be careful to answer these questions with complete honesty. This will be a tremendous help to you when trying to hire the right person for the job.

Qualities of a secretary:

A. Establish her worth
  1. What is your estimate of a secretary?
     a. What is her value to you? To the church?
     b. How should you treat her?
     c. How should others treat her?

  2. What skills does she need to possess to handle the job? What skills does she have?

  3. What type of individual are you looking for?
     a. Typist?
     b. Receptionist?

     c. Coworker?

     d. Part of your team?

     e. An extension of yourself?

B. Essential traits

1. A secretary's skills are only part of her total effectiveness; in your estimation, what makes up the other part?

C. The interview

1. What should we talk about?

2. What do I, as an employer, want to know about this prospective employee?

3. What questions could infringe on a person's "personal rights"?

4. What would an employee want to know about a prospective employer?

5. What will be the salary?

6. What are the fringe benefits?

7. What are the church's office hours?

D. Should I hire a member of my congregation?

E. Do I hire an inexperienced person I can train, or someone with experience?

After the interview, both the potential employee and the employer should take their time in making a decision.

As the employer, you should look for a balance between enthusiasm, experience, and education. Always check the references given to you by the prospective employee.

As the church grows, so will your staff. The following is a list of suggested hiring priorities for the growing church. Of course, this is merely a suggested list. Your staff will need to be added according to the definitive needs of your specific church.

Suggested Priorities in growth of a multiple staff:

1. Senior pastor
2. Church secretary, (serving as pastor's secretary, receptionist, bookkeeper)
3. First custodian
4. Youth or music minister
5. Second secretary (doubling as bookkeeper and secretary to the youth or music minister)
6. Music or youth minister
7. Third secretary (receptionist, doubling as music or youth secretary)
8. Children's pastor or Christian education director
9. Business manager
10. Bookkeeper
11. Visitation and pastoral care
12. Fourth secretary
13. Junior high minister
14. Second custodian
15. Fifth secretary
16. Singles minister
17. Sixth secretary
18. Senior citizens minister
19. College minister
20. Seventh secretary

Chapter 7

Church Finance:
Philosophy and Routine Procedures

C hurch finance is probably the most important subject in this area of the manual dealing with church administration. Pastors often do not know how to approach the area of finance in the church. Yet it is vital that every pastor know about the dynamics of church finance, the record keeping process, and the people's administration of money.

Your Philosophy of Church Finance

It has always been my philosophy never to touch any funds of the church except my own salary. However, I have always believed the pastor, as chairman of the board, has the responsibility to account for every cent of church money and report it to the corporation. Therefore, the pastor must take a very strong and active role in the administration of church finances.

In some instances, you may find yourself in a situation where the treasurer has put a hammerlock on church finance and has come to the conclusion that he is the only person responsible for the church's finances. In some places, you may become aware of the existence of tightfisted treasurers who dictate where money is or is not spent. This is a total misuse of the treasurer's office. The official board is actually the body which determines where all funds are spent. They are legally recognized as the board of trustees.

No pastor should ever feel threatened by members of the official board who want to know where church money is spent. That is their job. By the same token, a church board should not shirk their responsibility and defer these matters to a treasurer. The board must be led by the chairman, and they must act in unity when dealing with financial matters of the church.

The Treasurer

This office has been one of the most misunderstood areas of church work. Often, this is the result when treasurers have not been given definite directions concerning the job he/she is to fulfill.

The treasurer is the person who keeps a faithful record of all income and expenditures in the name of the church, and he/she carries out the instructions and wishes of the official board in all financial transactions. The treasurer, as an officer of the corporation, also has duties and obligations to government agencies. These duties should be well understood. If you have questions about the role of a treasurer in your state, either write to your district secretary or the Secretary of State's office and ask for the official requirements for a treasurer of a corporation.

The Chairman

Your role in financial matters should be viewed in your role as the chairman of the board, not as the pastor of the church. Over a short period of time, your board should be made aware of this important difference.

As chairman of the board, you are ultimately responsible for communication and accountability on all financial matters to your corporation. Therefore, it is your responsibility to know the financial policies, decisions, and accounting systems in your church.

As the chairman of the board, I have always operated on the philosophy that every member of the corporation not only *can* know about all financial matters concerning the church, but I feel they *should* know. Because of this, I have always given my people "too much" information. I have tried to answer all questions I feel they might have even before they are asked.

To do this, you must have excellent records and a full grasp of the financial picture at all times. If you ever get to the place you don't want to face financial responsibility and accountability, or if you want to hide financial information from your church, your pastoral days are numbered. People will forgive a pastor for almost anything, but they find it hard to ever forgive him for financial deceit or irresponsibility.

Your first step in becoming a good administrator of church finances is to ask for a detailed monthly financial statement. This statement should be reviewed at your monthly board meetings. I have always insisted upon a detailed breakdown of income and expenditures. I have also insisted the statements be balanced.

In a small church I asked the treasurer to list all transactions separately. In the larger church, I would ask the accountant to put all transactions into well-defined categories.

If the treasurer will not or cannot prepare a detailed statement, ask permission from the official board to work with the treasurer, authorizing you to prepare a financial statement through the church office (you). A board which has a sense of responsibility will be delighted to have a chairman who is interested in keeping good financial records. They may not, at first, want you to get much money yourself, but they will want you to be open and honest about church finances.

The following is a suggested monthly format for the financial report to the official board.

Your Church
Financial Report

For the Month of June

Bank Balance as of June 1:		$2,000
General Fund Income		
Tithes	$ 8,000	
Special Offerings	1,000	
Designated Giving		
Missions	2,000	
Youth	200	
Christian Education	400	
Women's Ministries	100	
Men's Ministries	100	
Building Fund	1,000	
Rental Income	150	
Misc. Income	50	
Total Income	$13,000	

<u>General Fund Disbursement</u>

Pastor's Salary & Benefits	$ 2,000	
Custodial Expense	400	
Loan Payments	1,000	
Interest On Loans	2,000	
Utilities	500	
Telephone	200	
Advertising	200	
Music Expense	100	
Office Expense & Petty Cash	250	
Guests	400	
Insurance	250	
Equipment	1,500	
Other	200	
(List all other expenses in categories)		
Transferred to Building Fund	1,000	
Total Disbursements	$10,000	
Income Over Disbursements		$3,000

Missions

Income	$ 2,000	
Disbursements	1,800	
Income Over Disbursements		200

Youth

Income	$ 200	
Disbursements	250	
Income Over Disbursements		(50)

Christian Education

Income	$ 400	
Disbursements	300	
Income Over Disbursements		100

Women's Ministries		
Income	$ 100	
Disbursements	200	
Income Over Disbursements		(100)
Men's Ministries		
Income	$ 100	
Disbursements	200	
Income Over Disbursements		(100)
Bank Balance: June 30 (General Fund)		$ 5,050
Bank Balance: (Building Fund)		$12,000

It is simple to make up a standard monthly form to be filled in by the treasurer each month. Use the basic form I have suggested as a working draft, then innovate line items as you need them.

Central Checking System

I have learned over the years to consolidate all of the church funds through one checkbook. I have suggested a separate account for the building funds because it is good to place the building fund into an interest-bearing account. However, it is good church administration to run all funds and checks through the general ledger. Obviously, if you have several small accounts, you are going to have difficulty in keeping an accurate financial record.

Provide funds for emergencies through a petty cash fund. Always demand receipts and keep an accurate record of expenses these funds are used for. Also make certain that departments or ministries are charged properly when they use petty cash.

In order to have a unified checking system, the pastor must be able to sign checks. If this procedure is not approved, the board will have to authorize other people who are readily accessible to sign checks.

I have found, over the years, that it is wise for the official board to require two signatures on all checks. Sometimes it is inconvenient, but it is a great discipline. I have said that the pastor should not touch church money, and I firmly believe this is true. However, the pastor **does** need to have a constant awareness of the financial health of the church. In order to enhance this awareness, I believe the pastor should countersign all checks. Officers of the corporation should be authorized to sign checks in the absence of the pastor. With double signatures, you automatically build trust with your congregation.

Control of Expenditures

This is one of the most trying areas of financial administration, but it is absolutely vital for maintaining good control. When, how much, and where the church can be financially obligated is an educational process. There are basically two systems of control you need to establish: In-House Control and Credit Control.

In House Control: Requesting Funds

If you as pastor or anyone in church leadership need to obtain a check from the treasurer, the individual making the request should fill out a check request form. A sample form is printed below.

A supply of these forms should be printed, then placed in two or three designated areas where church personnel can have easy access to them.

```
┌─────────────────────────────────────────────────┐
│                  REQUEST FOR                    │
│   ☐ FUNDS                      ☐ REFUND         │
├─────────────────────────────────────────────────┤
│                                                 │
│   Item Needed_____     │
│   Amount Needed _____     │
│   When Needed _____     │
│   Requested By _____     │
│   Make Check Payable To _____     │
│                                                 │
│                   _____  │
│                                                 │
│   IF REFUND REQUEST, PLEASE ATTACH RECEIPT(S)   │
│                                                 │
└─────────────────────────────────────────────────┘
```

All requests for church funds should be accompanied by some supporting record. This is not because you distrust people, but because it is the only equitable, practical way to keep a set of books. Challenge your board to begin to conduct the Lord's business and the church's financial program in a professional way. Sell the treasurer on the idea that simple procedures which are systematically followed will make the job easier in the long run. Also, these procedures are helpful when there is a change in personnel.

Credit Control

Church charge accounts should be consistently monitored. It is a good idea to have the official board approve the people who are to be authorized to use the church's charge accounts.

Most businesses will demand copies of the signatures of those people who are authorized to charge merchandise on the church account. You cannot be protected 100 percent, but you should carefully review all charges to the church so you can immediately correct any obvious misuse of the church's credit.

Giving Records

The financial strength of your church is based on the spiritual motivation of your people in their tithes and offerings. In order to encourage the people and show them how important their faithful giving is to the church, you must maintain good individual records for them.

When your church is small, it is not difficult to keep all records by hand. When numerical growth warrants computerization, you will need other kinds of accounting procedures.

For many years I effectively used the annual tithing envelope box system. This system is available for a nominal fee through several religious supply houses. Christian bookstores usually handle these as well.

Your treasurer, together with some volunteers, should assign every tithing unit in the church a box of envelopes. If a husband and wife tithe together, they should receive only one box. I was very strong in my insistence that children from the fourth grade up receive their own boxes and tithing numbers as a teaching tool for giving.

When people coming into the church request tithing envelopes or a tithing number, it is very simple to add the name and number of the individual to the tithing ledger and issue them a box of envelopes with their number stamped on it. Because many people will come into the church throughout the year, it is necessary to order a surplus of tithing envelopes.

Prior to every Sunday service, you will want to make sure there is an adequate supply of generic offering envelopes available for those who have forgotten or misplaced their numbered envelopes.

By using numerically-assigned envelopes, either at the end of each quarter or once a year you will be able to total the giving record for each person and send them that record for tax purposes. The people of your congregation will appreciate this service.

I am adamant about providing my people good service in financial information. The cost for purchasing envelopes, recording the giving, and sending out the tax return information is small in comparison to the return of the church's investment. I shall never forget the overwhelming response I got the first year we mailed out the people's giving records (by January 15) for the previous year's giving.

Make giving important by providing the giver all the support and encouragement you can. If you're not slothful in church business, people will take their giving seriously.

The giving record ledger is a numbered book which contains ample columns and space for each individual giving unit. You and your treasurer should assign a close-mouthed, willing person the task of taking the envelopes and entering the figures in the ledger each week.

Because of the importance of this information, the giving ledger should be kept in a safe place on the church's premises.

All the envelopes for the year should be stored in a box as a back-up system in case something happens to the ledger. You may be called upon by the IRS from time to time to verify the giving of an individual. Financial records are fast becoming the most scrutinized part of church work.

Banking Procedures

After each offering is taken, the money should be counted and receipted by at least two very responsible people in your church. When money is taken out of offering envelopes, the figures should be checked against the amount written on the outside of the envelope.

Sunday school offerings should be counted separately. This is usually handled by the Sunday school treasurer, then recounted and verified by the people who fill out the bank deposits.

The following steps should be taken by those counting the offerings:

1. Remove money or checks from the offering envelopes. Check the amount recorded on the front of the envelope against what was actually inside. If the amounts vary, make corrections on the envelope for the benefit of the person who will make ledger entries for individual giving.

2. If there is a check without an envelope, simply fill out an envelope for the individual or place the person's name and amount given on a piece of paper.

3. Band all the envelopes and giving receipts together and put them in a safe, pre-arranged place so the giving recorder can enter the information from the envelopes in the ledger.

4. Count the bills and change separately.

5. List all checks on a bank deposit slip. Make sure the deposit slip is in duplicate or triplicate form.

6. Complete all necessary information on the deposit slip.

7. Place the original deposit slip in a bank bag along with the money and checks.

8. Give a duplicate deposit slip to the treasurer. If the deposit slip is made in triplicate, keep a copy for yourself.

9. Keep the bank deposit in a safe place until it can be taken to the bank. I think the use of a night deposit is a wise procedure.

10. The treasurer or authorized representative should make the deposit that night or the next day. The treasurer should immediately make any corrections if there are counting errors on the deposit.

Budgeting

I have always believed in a church budget even when the church was small. Budgets establish priorities. Budgets anticipate projects to help you plan programs. Budgets help the board to consider the entire year and save time in later meetings. Budgets help keep the church's financial programs balanced.

As a rule of thumb, budgets should be divided almost equally between administration, debt servicing, and church operations. These three areas include:

Administration: basically salaries.

Debt Servicing: principal and interest payments.

Church Operations: what it costs to keep the church functioning with all its needs; i.e., utilities, supplies, department expenses, etc.

Missions is designated giving, as is the building fund, and these funds should not be figured in the general budget unless a certain percentage of your total budget goes to these areas.

Near the end of each calendar year, I prepared a proposed budget for the official board. It was not elaborate, but it was clear. I left my salary open for them to discuss and fill in when completing the budget process. A budget should list all major areas of expense in the church. Projected costs for new programs and/or projects should be included in each of these areas.

The board should understand that the budget is a guide to be followed, but that it will possibly need to be changed from time to time during the year to accommodate unforeseen expenses and/ or unusual income.

Further directions for financial reporting is explained in chapter 9, "The Annual Business Meeting."

Chapter 8

The Official Board

Almost every pastor of a sovereign Assemblies of God church is instantly thrust into three basic positions. Each position is different, yet all three overlap.

When you were elected, you became pastor of the congregation, president of the corporation, and administrator of the church. In order to be an effective pastor and administrator, it is necessary to be effective in your role as the president of the board of directors--*chairman of the official board*.

The Personnel and Function of the Official Board

From the very beginning, many pastors have real difficulty chairing boards and committees. I believe most problems stem from attitudes which have grown out of horror stories about some ghastly board meeting which ran until 4 a.m., and ended in a church split. Some problems also stem from generalizations made about "tough," "hard," or "carnal" board members.

Every pastor should take the time to cultivate friendships with each board member. I make no bones about it. These men work closely with me, therefore, for the good of the church I seek to stay close to them.

Jesus had a small group He chose to work through. He developed a very close relationship with these men. He knew their strengths and their weaknesses. As Jesus did with His disciples, the wise pastor will spend time cultivating strong, healthy relationships with board members.

Who becomes a member of the board is out of your control because the corporation (the active, voting members of the church) choose who will represent them during a called business meeting. The Constitution and By-Laws of your local church spell out how the members of the board are to be elected, what are to be their qualifications, what is the term of office, and how meetings are called. Study your Constitution and By-Laws carefully in the sections dealing with the official board. You are bound by law to operate by those directives.

The size of the church's official board will vary. There can be as few as three members or as many as the local church feels necessary to smoothly run the church. One church I was in had 21 board members.

In addition to, or sometimes within the membership of the board, are the church officers: *the president, vice president, secretary, and treasurer.* The Constitution and By-Laws also spells out how these officers are to be elected.

I am aware of two pastors who could not find a Constitution

and By-Laws for their church when they were elected. They immediately asked that the suggested Constitution and By-Laws for sovereign Assemblies of God churches, supplied by the District Office or General Council, be adapted as a temporary document. These pastors then went to work preparing a Constitution and By-Laws for their churches. If you find yourself in this same situation, the method those pastors used is very good.

The official board carries out all legal matters of the church. These people possess the power to act on official documents and properties, and they also have the oversight of all monies.

In addition to physical and fiscal matters, the official board serves as collective spiritual advisors to the pastor. Your official board should not be considered a threat. This is a body which will share your burdens and protect you from taking full responsibility for official decisions. I have always enjoyed working through boards and committees.

Chairing the Official Board

Between all board meetings, keep a small notebook handy to jot down items you consider necessary for board action. A few days prior to the scheduled board meeting (most churches have these on a monthly basis), you should use this list to help prepare the agenda. You should follow a basic rule throughout your ministry: **NO AGENDA, NO MEETING**.

Agendas are written guides to determine the matters for discussion. If you don't have an agenda, the meeting will run you instead of you running the meeting. The agenda should be typed and given to board members as they arrive at the meeting. My suggested agenda is as follows:

    1. **CALL TO ORDER**: "I am calling the Official Board of ---- church to order."

2. **DEVOTIONS AND PRAYER**

3. **AGENDA**: Say, "You have the agenda before you. Does anyone have any new business to add which is not covered on the agenda?" If someone does, say, "Please put this item down as number ----." When the men have finished making additions, say, "All in favor of adapting this agenda as a guide but not as a rule say 'aye.' Opposed by the same sign."

Establishing an agenda at the beginning tells you how many items you have and what is on members' minds. It discourages someone from bringing up a "hot" item right at the last. It also mentally prepares the board for what they will be dealing with during the meeting.

4. **MINUTES**:   "I will now ask the secretary to read the minutes of our last meeting. Are there any corrections or additions to the reading of the minutes? All in favor of receiving the minutes as read and corrected (if there were corrections), as Official Record Copy say 'aye.' Opposed, 'nay.' So ordered."

5. **FINANCIAL REPORT**

6. **PASTOR'S REPORT**: Here I place items about the general health of the church, matters of membership, reports about departments in the church, personal plans, and needs I perceive.

Agenda items under the Pastor's Report might include:
   a. Numerical and Spiritual Growth
   b. Proposed Men's Ministries Program
   c. Report from the District Council
   d. Proposed Revival Series

7. **FINANCIAL MATTERS**: This is self-explanatory, but make sure you have done your homework when you propose purchases or when reporting on costs of pro-

grams. Give a detailed breakdown (how the money will be raised.or how it affects the general fund). Most pastors who have problems with boards do so because they are not always up front or specific about money matters.

I am saying that pastors have a tendency to be "wishful thinkers" about money. The Bible says we are to be sharp in business--not slothful. We are to "count the cost."

Many boards have turned excessively conservative because they have been asked to make decisions in the past which are based on either wrong or no information. Don't guess what things are going to cost. Find out before the meeting.

Don't say, "A good used van shouldn't cost us over $2,000." Instead, say, "I have prepared some figures for you on the cost of a used van. Courtesy Chevrolet has two. They are 3 years old, have 40,000 miles, and are in good condition. We can purchase either one for $2,395."

Always give your board realistic, provable, and complete financial data for their decision making. You will begin to build their trust in what you say. Many preachers are not viewed as good businessmen because they have not disciplined themselves to tend to the business side of the church.

8. **REFERRALS FROM PAST MEETINGS**
9. **NEW BUSINESS**
10. **ADJOURNMENT**

Recording the Meeting

The secretary is legally responsible for keeping minutes. Often the secretary of a board is not skilled in these areas. As the chairman, you must make sure that good, detailed minutes are kept and recorded.

Work closely with the secretary and ask that a copy of the minutes be submitted to you as soon as possible. Every official action should be shown as motioned, seconded, and passed (or defeated). Diplomatically work out a way to review the minutes and make corrections and additions with the secretary before the minutes are typed and sent to the board members.

Make certain an official book of minutes is kept by the secretary. A copy of all minutes should be kept at the church for your instant referral.

Conducting the Meeting

You are among friends, but you are conducting business. Never forget that. Your attitude will determine the spirit of most meetings. You should chair a meeting with the attitude that every member has a right to his/her opinion.

Be fair and evenhanded. Give opportunity for discussion. Be sensitive to when the discussion is becoming redundant. Deliberately **move** the meeting along, but do not **force** the meeting along. Be objective.

Do not take criticism about the church or departments as personal attacks. Take criticisms as observations made by duly elected representatives of the church. Realize that these criticisms could lead to improvements in the church.

Determine prior to any meeting not to allow anyone or anything make you lose your temper. You will sometimes need to be firm, but refuse to allow yourself to lose control.

In small groups it is not necessary to be formal about parliamentary procedure. However, you should follow it. You should study and adhere to the basic rules. Main motions and amendments should be understood. Motions should be stated, voted upon, and then recorded in proper order. I have always enjoyed using *"Robert's Rules of Order."* As you are going to be chairing many meetings, it is necessary at the very beginning to learn and practice some of the basic rules until they become second nature.

In official board meetings, follow the agenda. Assist in forming motions and receiving amendments. Then allow for discussion and debate. After discussion take care of the amendments in order, then state the main motion as amended. Be very flexible about parliamentary procedure in board meetings, but insist on following the procedures when it is time to make official decisions.

Practical Considerations for Chairmen

DO:

· Start the meeting on time if there is a quorum. This teaches by example.

· Prepare resolutions you are bringing to the board in advance. This saves time trying to frame a complicated resolution on the spot. Give the board members a typed copy of your proposed resolution and supporting data.

· Rotate your men in opening and closing the meetings in prayer.

· Allow plenty of time for discussion on difficult issues. Draw discussions to a close by saying, "I would like to ask each board member to tell us briefly what you think should be done." This clarifies their thinking and when you come to the last person, you have given the signal it is time to vote.

· Use secret ballots when personalities are involved or if very sensitive issues are being decided.

· Remind board members often that board meetings are confidential and opinions expressed should not be discussed with anyone, even their wives. They will not feel free to be open and honest if they think what they say will be repeated outside the board meeting.

DON'T:

· Hide anything from your board which will affect the church in any way.

· Threaten to resign if you don't have your way. Resignations should come from prayerful direction, not from difficult situations. Before resigning, talk to your district superintendent.

· Show favoritism to one board member above another.

· Tell close friends what one of your board members said in a board meeting. Practice what you preach. Board meetings are confidential.

Your board is a great gift. Lead with spiritual wisdom. Use the board as a means for spiritual growth and harmony. Build a camaraderie and sense of security which will allow them to say or discuss anything in Christian love. When a board meeting is over, you should all be able to say, "The board decided and we are united."

I have made it a practice before each annual business meeting to talk to the deacon or deacons who are going to be voted on with the rest of the board present. You might say, "Brother ----, you are going to be voted upon. No one knows what might happen in business meetings. I would like to know how you would react if the people decided not to return you to office?" This, of course, will give you and the board some assurance of how the deacon feels. It also helps him to act maturely if he is not returned to his position.

In all my years of conducting board meetings I cannot remember a time when I didn't feel positive about the outcome of a board meeting--even when we had to deal with very unpleasant situations. I can assure you that, overall, the times you spend in board meetings will be some of the most gratifying hours you will spend in pastoring.

Chapter 9

The Annual Business Meeting

our goals for the Annual Business Meeting are three-fold:

1) *to give a full report of all relevant activities and data covering the past year,*

2) *to conduct elections and business competently, and in a spirit of unity; and*

3) *to build faith in your people as you work together to meet challenges of the coming year.*

This particular meeting is often feared by pastors because it is the only time the congregation sees the pastor in the role of chairman of the corporation.

The secret to having a productive business meeting is to be well prepared.

The Annual Report

The annual report should cover every major area of the church. It should have a heavy emphasis on financial detail, and should be neatly typed and attractive in appearance.

Your annual report says a great deal more than the information you present. It tells the people how seriously you take your responsibility. It also tells them whether you are careless or careful about business. But perhaps the most important thing it tells them is how open and honest you are about financial matters.

The annual report is a real reflection of your integrity as a minister.

The cover can be a good quality, colored paper. Neat lettering, stating the name and address of the church, the title "*Annual Business Report*," and the year the report covers should be placed in an attractive design across the front.

The first page of my report has usually been titled, "*The Year in Review*." In this section of the report I list every unusual and interesting event which has occurred that year. I also include the dates on which these events occurred. This information includes all special guests (both pulpit and music), church anniversaries, special productions, and new programs which have been instituted. It is always amazing how much activity which has taken place during the year has been forgotten by annual report time.

The next page should be "*The Pastor's Report*." From my perspective, I write a miniature "state of the church" report. I let my congregation know where I feel the church is spiritually, financially, and numerically.

I then thank a number of people who were obviously significant in my life--my family, my wife, the boards and committees I worked with on a regular basis, and other individuals worthy of recognition. Be careful to thank only those people who made obviously unique contributions (other than financial) to the church throughout the year.

Report next on members who died, and finally, give a personal report on your ministry--the number of times you preached, the weddings you performed, the committees you have served on, etc. Your people need to know the scope of your ministry within the last year.

The next few pages will contain the financial reports. Begin the annual report with the *STATEMENT OF CONDITION*. It should look something like the following:

STATEMENT OF CONDITION
AS OF DECEMBER 31

ASSETS

Cash Balance
> Cash in Checking Account
> Cash in Savings Account
> Cash in Building Fund
>> Total Cash:

Property
> Church Land
> Church Buildings
> Church Furnishings
> Any Other Real Properties
> Vehicles
>> Total Property:

>> Total Assets:

Your assets on real property should be the actual amounts paid, not the fair market value or new appraisals.

LIABILITIES

Mortgages Payable
> Loan on Church
> Bonds, if any
> Loans on Other Properties
> Loans from Individuals
>> Total Liabilities:

Net Worth:

You need an accurate statement of condition each year. Not only will your members feel more comfortable when they receive this information, but this will also be helpful should you need to borrow money from a lending institution in the future.

Go into great detail when giving the financial report. Use the basic format for the suggested monthly financial reports to the official board and simply total annual figures for all the line items under "*Income and Disbursements.*" This includes reports on your separate departments as well.

On the next page of the Annual Report, put your proposed church budget for the coming year. The budget should not be too detailed, but it should include the pastor's salary, secretary's salary (if applicable), and funds to be used for securing evangelists and for presenting special programs. It should also include funds to be spent on advertising, missions, utilities, loan payments, phone costs, office expenses, church operating expenses, music, transportation, Christian education, etc.

The rest of your annual report should be reports about various church departments. It is a good discipline and motivation for department heads when they know they will be asked to give annual reports about their areas. These reports also teach your congregation that you are effectively using people in places of leadership.

The Annual Business Meeting

Read your Constitution and By-Laws to determine how business meetings are to be called. In most churches it is to be announced a minimum of two Sundays prior to the meeting. Other By-Laws call for written notices.

Also, determine if there are any restrictions about changing the church's Constitution and By-Laws. Most of the time you cannot change the Constitution unless written notice of the proposed change is given to members some time before the Annual Business Meeting. In some churches, members cannot change the By-Laws unless certain criteria is met.

Announce any deadline members have to meet if they wish to submit resolutions affecting the Constitution and/or By-Laws well in advance. The proposed resolutions should be in the hands of the secretary by the stated deadline.

You should also post a list of all eligible voting members in the church lobby. This should be done two or three Sundays prior to the Annual Business Meeting. This gives time to make any corrections to the list well in advance.

On the night of the business meeting, have one or two people check the membership roster as each member comes in. Have them give a copy of the Annual Report to the member as he/she arrives. Using this method will help the chairman of your teller's committee quickly tally the number of legal voting members present at the meeting.

In the official board meeting immediately prior to the Annual Business Meeting, appoint tellers. These people should not be deacons who will be voted upon, but they must be respected and trusted people in the membership. Appoint a chairman, making certain he prepares enough ballots for the meeting.

Carefully read the main points of parliamentary procedure from your *Rules of Order*. Be certain about basic rules, such as amendments, point of order, etc. It would be good to take a copy of "*Robert's Rules of Order*" (or whatever rules you choose to use) with you to every meeting.

You will need the following materials in hand when you call the meeting to order:

- a copy of the minutes of your last Annual Business Meeting;
- a copy of the church's Constitution and By-Laws;
- your parliamentary guide;
- an agenda;
- resolutions from the official board (if any); and
- an overhead or blackboard to report on elections.

You begin the meeting by stating that you are calling the meeting to order. Then you can say, "Our first order of business is the reading of the Scripture verses and prayer for God's special blessing and guidance upon all our proceedings." You should plan to pray yourself, or ask a venerated elder who is not involved in the election process to do so.

After prayer, announce the informal guidelines you will follow during the meeting. I say something like:

"Now friends, I want to state a few guidelines we should follow if we are going to have a good business meeting. To me, our attitude during this meeting is more important than the business we discuss. I want you to feel free to discuss any subject or ask any question. I want you to voice your opinion, but as Spirit-filled believers, it is incumbent upon us to maintain a spirit of love and cooperation. None of us should feel superior to anyone else.

"I will respect your opinion, but it is your opinion. It is no better or no worse than someone else's. We may not be sure your opinion is right, but we can certainly be sure when your attitude is not right. I can disagree with you, but, as a Christian, I cannot be disagreeable or rude.

"I am also asking that each member stand and be recognized by the chair before speaking. I will be following parliamentary procedure informally. Thus we can be assured everything will be done decently and in order. If we follow these guidelines, I am sure the Lord's blessing will be upon us.

"The official board has appointed the following people to serve as our tellers for this meeting. [Read the names]. I would entertain a motion to ratify the appointment of these individuals to serve as tellers. Is there a second? Any questions? All in favor say 'aye,' all opposed by the same sign.

"We will now have the reading of the minutes of our last year's Annual Business Meeting."

The secretary of the corporation should begin by reading the minutes. After the secretary is finished, ask for any additions or corrections to the reading of the minutes, making note of these. Then entertain a motion to receive the minutes of the last meeting as read (or as corrected).

If you are going to have elections, it is wise to move directly to elections and intersperse your reports while the tellers count the ballots. You could let your people know that this is the way you, as chairman, wish to handle this. As this is in opposition to some rules, you would need to have a motion made and seconded to suspend the rules and call for elections to be interspersed with reports. When made, the motion should be voted on.

Before the election of pastor or deacon, you will need to do several things. First, ask for a report from the chairman of the teller's committee as to how many voting members are in attendance. As there are a few church By-Laws which call for a quorum, knowing the quorum has been met is of utmost importance.

Before each office is voted on, have the secretary of the corporation read the qualifications for that office. Tell the people that you will declare any person elected on the nominating ballot if they receive enough votes to be elected. Then have the tellers hand out the ballots. Instruct the people to vote, then collect the ballots.

While the tellers tabulate the votes, continue with the meeting--reading reports and resolutions.

Ask the chairman of the teller's committee to bring the tabulation of each ballot to the secretary for reporting. Ask the secretary to hand you the results of each ballot as they come in. Interrupt the reading of reports each time to give a report on the ballots cast. Do not list the number of votes cast for each person on the first (nominating) ballot. If the person nominated receives enough to be elected, declare that person elected.

If the office of pastor is to be voted on, turn the chair to the vice-chairman or an officer who has been designated by the official board prior to the meeting. Leave the meeting and go to your office while this election is taking place. Ask to be summoned as soon as the election for pastor is completed.

If you are returned to office, thank the people graciously. If you are not reelected, accept this vote with grace and assure the people you will be praying God will lead them.

It is wisdom to have the election of pastor at the end of the meeting. If you are re-elected to office, the meeting ends on a high note. If you are not, there is not much point in trying to conduct business.

If possible, I recommend that a separate business meeting be held for the sole purpose of voting on the office of pastor.

After all elections are completed, you are ready for resolutions. When the official board has resolutions which the members have recommended, have the secretary of the board read the recommendation and move its adoption and ask for a second.

After receiving a second, then ask for discussion. If the discussion is vigorous, the chair should keep a balance of pro and con. If someone has just spoken for the motion, you should ask the next person who is recognized if he is going to speak against the motion. If the person is also for the motion, ask if there is someone who wishes to speak against the motion. If no one wishes to speak in the negative, allow the next member to speak in favor.

It is your job to keep people on the subject. If someone offers an amendment to the motion, then keep the debate on the amendment. If there is an amendment to the amendment (there can be no more than two amendments on the floor at any given time), ask for debate on the amendment to the amendment. After the amendments have been voted on, present the main motion as amended for a final vote.

Debate should end when it is apparent people are saying the same thing over and over. Be very patient in allowing debate. However, when you think it is obviously time to vote, tell the members you would entertain a motion for calling for the question. If there is such a motion and it is passed, move immediately to vote on the motion.

When resolutions and/or any pending business from other meetings have been dealt with, ask if there is any new business.

Usually new business takes one of two forms. New business to some people means an opportunity to ask questions or state opinions. Answer questions and receive opinions the best you can.

The other way new business comes to the floor is when someone says, "I would like to make a motion." You would say, "Please state your motion."

If the motion is to change the Constitution and By-Laws, you would have to declare the motion out of order if the Constitution and By-Laws contain a procedure that makes it impossible to change it without previous notice. You would then remind the members that opportunity had been given and announcements made concerning when resolutions affecting the Constitution and By-Laws could be received. Encourage them to remember this procedure laid down by their own rules and regulations.

If the resolution is in order, ask for a second. If there is no second to the motion after a significant time (15 to 20 seconds), you would then say, "The motion is lost for the want of a second." If there is a second to the motion, say, "Would the brother or sister who presented this motion like to be the first to speak in favor of the motion?"

Go through the debate. When everyone is finished speaking and they are ready to vote, explain what the motion concerns. If it is a technical motion, ask the person making the motion to jot it down and give it to the secretary so you will get it right.

Just prior to adjournment, after all the elections, reports, and new business, I say, "I would like to acknowledge those who have previously served our church." Call the names of deacons and officers not returned to office for any reason. Make some positive and sincere remarks about each one.

When these recognitions are complete, then ask the newly-elected deacons and officers to join you at the front. Assure the people of your willingness to work with these new officers, then have each of those elected say a brief word in response. It is also good, if the meeting does not run too late, to introduce the rest of the board by having them join you at the front as well.

When all of this has been completed, ask for a motion and a second to adjourn the meeting. You can have those in favor of adjournment to rise.

Make a few brief comments on the good meeting. Then ask everyone to pray with you for the newly-elected board members, the other actions taken which will have significant effect on the congregation, and the continued blessing of God on the church.

Chapter 10

The Art of Preaching

To even touch the subject of preaching in one chapter is like asking someone to write a 500 word essay on the topic of *The Origin, Nature, and Destiny of the Universe*!

To me, preaching cannot really be taught. It is an art which is learned over many years of fervent trial and error.

I have now been preaching well over 25 years, and I have spent these many years majoring on my preaching ministry. Yet if you asked what I want to learn during my next 25 years, I would tell you that I would like to learn how to *really* preach. I do not believe a person ever masters this art. The challenge is always there. After all, it is through the foolishness of preaching that people come to God.

What I will attempt to do in this chapter is condense what I have learned during my 25 plus years of preaching into a few words. You must understand from the very beginning, however, that there is no shortcut to the agony and the ecstacy of preaching. I can only relate to you how I preach, and should you learn even one thing from this chapter you should count yourself fortunate.

If you are like me, about the time you think you have learned something about preaching you will find yourself humbly rising from the dust after falling flat on your face.

In preparing to preach, I always ask myself four basic questions about the occasion where I will preach. How I answer these questions then determines my process of preparation.

The first question I deal with is: *Is my message supposed to meet a specific need?*

The way you answer this will determine the direction of your preaching. I am convinced the Holy Spirit will direct a man of God in knowing the *real* needs of a person, a congregation, or a community.

There is nothing mysterious concerning what you should preach about. God's Spirit will always lead if you are open. There will be times when you are certain the need is personal and that your entire sermon is to be directed to one unknown person. There have been times when I have literally wept during my time of preparation because of the burden God had given me for an unknown person.

There might also be times when you will be impressed to preach a series of doctrinal sermons, or perhaps an exegetical series. However God burdens your heart, that is what you should preach.

A pastor must learn how to preach every style and kind of sermon. *Should a pastor preach topically, exegetically, homiletically, evangelistically, or doctrinally?* The answer is

"*yes*" to all of these styles. I do not believe a pastor can meet the spiritual needs of his people by preaching only one style. Do not lock yourself into a "proclaiming" or a "sharing" style. Do not lock yourself into *any* singular style. Learn to use them all functionally. By doing so, you will be able to meet all the needs represented by the various personalities in your congregation.

The reason for preaching is to bring God into people's needs in such a way that He is allowed to make a difference in their lives. Everywhere Jesus went He went with a clear purpose in view. Every time Jesus spoke He spoke to a need in the lives of His listeners. Jesus could have impressed everyone by His superintelligence and His divine vocabulary. Yet Jesus chose to speak the language of the people, not the language of the theologians.

As I prepare to preach, I first prepare my heart to see the spiritual and practical needs of my people. I must be impressed by the Holy Spirit to expound on a certain topic.

There have been times when I have felt called to preach "policy sermons"--making a clear statement as to where the church stands on contemporary issues which are impacting the church. At other times I have been impressed to preach a series on the family or to bring a message which will do nothing more than edify or encourage our body of believers. At all times, I preach what the Spirit impresses upon me to preach.

My problem has never been *what* to preach. My problem has been in knowing what I was to preach about when--according to God's timing. If you stay open to the leading of the Spirit--the One who leads us into all truth--you will always know the need of your congregation at that hour. Once the need is clear, you will then have the proper motivation and discipline to meet that need through your preaching.

After determining the need, you are ready to answer the second question: *Is the message supported by the Bible and in harmony with biblical principles?*

You are a gospel preacher. Therefore, you must be a Bible preacher. Our preaching is not to be done within the framework of human response to human need. Our preaching is to be done in the framework of a Divine response through human instrumentality. Your task is to build a strong biblical support base for your subject.

When the message is topical and contemporary, I carefully study the basic biblical principles which impact the subject. Of course, when the subject is doctrinal and exegetical, the need for cross-referencing is obvious. *Why do I go through this discipline?* Because if a preacher is not very careful, he will begin to use the Scriptures to support his theories rather than digesting and then imparting God's truths--even when these truths come into conflict with human theory. Study the Scriptures first. Then you will be able to study men's thoughts and interpretations without being misled.

After building a scriptural foundation, I then seek to build a superstructure of application where people live. The Word must never be compromised by the application. However the application must be discernable and practical.

It is at this juncture many preachers become lazy. If you want to become an effective preacher, you must be a student of life. In order to do this, you must have the desire and the will to collect insights from life.

This is done by observing and listening to what has happened and what is happening. It is good to write down what I call "flashes of insight." Thought and observations which really excite you will have a tendency to do the same for others.

Of course, the greatest source of spiritual and practical insights comes from books. The resource of books is one of life's greatest gifts. The best of the best is available to all preachers through publications. You must face certain realities with books. I will give you some of my secrets.

1. I have certain authors who give me great insights. Just as you have favorite preachers who deeply affect you, you will find that some writers will do the same thing. Build your own group of favorite authors; read materials by those who speak powerfully to you.

Do not be embarrassed to accept the fact that there are popular writers who do not make an impact on you. For instance, I have a terrible time getting anything out of Spurgeon, Talmage, and Meyer. On the other hand, I gain a tremendous amount of material from G.H. Morrrison, J. Stuart Holden, Clovis Chappell, G. Campbell Morgan, and the Keswick preachers. But that is me. You will have others who will deeply affect your preaching.

2. Learn to read sermon books fast and become skilled in discovering the "flashes of insight" which really "turn you on." I read a book recently entitled *A Day In the Lord's Court*, by J.B. Chapman. Among the flashes of insight I underlined were these:

> *The old must die, the young may die. Time is the dressing room, eternity is the real stage of action, and death is the door which opens between the dressing room and the stage. Death cannot touch my spirit. His doubt was not sinful, it was just paralyzing.*

These statements were real food for thought. Some day I will weave them into a message. Works of fiction can also provide this same benefit at times.

3. Learn to study theology by disciplining yourself to

understand clearly what the writer is saying. To read Charles Hodge or Charles Finney and to really understand them is not just a challenge, it is a necessary discipline. Carefully study at least one major theological work a year to stretch your brain and force you to think in new patterns. This is vital for giving depth to your pulpit ministry.

4. Read humanistic literature in the right way. Read liberal theologians, philosophers, and psychologists not to deepen your understanding of the Bible and theology; read them to deepen your insight into human behavior and thought.

I read several of these books each year. Though they are miles away from my beliefs, they are often right on target about the people I preach to and the world in which I live. Choose to ignore their religious arguments; simply retain their valid insights.

While you are reading these materials, jot down all the thoughts and insights which are not contrary to the Bible. After reviewing your scriptural references, making your own personal insights and compiling pertinent material from books, you are now ready to prepare your actual sermon.

Your goal in preparing a message must be a resounding "yes" to the third question: *Is the message I have prepared clear to me and will it be clear to my listeners on all points?*

In order to make my messages clear, I discipline myself to prepare the sermon in the presence of an invisible person who does not have the slightest idea about the subject I am going to address. I have to constantly remind myself that I cannot assume the people I am preaching to know what I am preaching about.

If I use a Bible story such as David and Goliath to build a message on, I take the time to quickly tell that familiar story. You would be shocked at how unfamiliar the story of David and Goliath might be to a general audience. You must establish a common point of knowledge and understanding so you can take all your listeners from the known to the unknown.

After introducing your message clearly, it is your task to arrange the body of the sermon in a logical sequence. This does two things. First, *it keeps your listeners on track, enabling them to follow as you lead them in truth.* Second, *it keeps you on track and gives you the ability to easily discard extraneous material.*

As I read over the raw material, I watch for major themes emerging from the data. If I am preaching on the subject of repentance, I seek for major themes within the subject. Sometimes a sentence in a book triggers my thought pattern and I develop one of my major points from that sentence. Always be aware of sequence.

Where am I with this subject? Where do I want to go with it to meet the needs of the people? These are two very important questions you will need to answer.

Your major themes concerning repentance might be as simple as: *Who should repent? Why should they repent? How do they repent? and When should they repent?* Be careful! The simple outlines are often the most difficult to develop with clarity. For instance, under the first theme, *"Who should repent?"* you must clarify the nature of sin as well as the nature of man in a fresh, interesting way. You must be elementary enough to make sure your invisible person can understand, yet you must be profound enough to hold the interest and also teach the mature Christian. *You have to learn how to be profound through simplicity!*

The major themes will create the skeleton on which to hang vital truths. There are usually two or three vital truths under each major theme. These vital truths should be closely tied together; the truths under each major theme should flow in logical sequence.

When you have your major themes and vital truths supporting these themes, flesh out your sermon by using down-to-earth applications. After building a fine homiletical structure, you must make the sermon live by asking yourself a very pivotal question: *What difference will each of these themes make in the lives of my people when they are not in church?*

We are preaching living truth. Living truth is lived through lives. Your sermon may end, but *the truth of the sermon begins after it is preached.* Remember, the man who knows nothing needs the truth you are preaching. What fundamental change will take place in the person who has the need you are addressing?

So much preaching does not make any earthly difference. This is because the preacher has not prepared the sermon to make any difference now. "So heavenly it's no earthly good" is a very time-worn cliche which certainly describes a lot of preaching today! Therefore, you must stay true to the homiletical structure of your message. Flesh it out with insights, illustrations, and scriptural applications that affect people today. Make the sermon live in a way that people are able to follow you easily and be able to relate to every point you are making.

Last, and I believe most important, when it is all said and done, you must be able to say "yes" to the following questions: *Am I deeply moved by the message I have prepared? Would I like to hear it from someone else? Do I think it is one of the most important and life-changing messages I have ever heard?*

If I do not honestly feel that way about the sermon I have prepared, I go back and do it over. If I am not excited about it, I will certainly not be able to motivate others to listen to it all the way through, let alone be able to excite them enough so they will practice its truths in their everyday lives.

You may ask, "Do you feel that what you are preaching is the most important thing you have ever preached every time you preach?" My answer to that question is always a resounding "yes."

I cannot remember a time during my preparation when I did not think that the truth I was preparing for delivery was the most life-changing, exciting revelation I had received to that point. If I do not feel that way, I seek God until I do. I cannot imagine wasting the time of any group with anything less than the best that the Holy Spirit can accomplish through me by preparation.

Entire books are written on the art of preaching; many are very good. However, preaching is a living process which no one can really explain on paper.

After you have prepared your sermon the best that you know how, there has to come a special ministry of the Holy Spirit upon both the preacher and the listeners--a type of "divine chemistry." When it does not happen, you feel like you have lost the World Series by an error in the 9th inning. When it does happen, you will feel better than any quarterback who has ever won the Super Bowl by a brilliant pass in the last second. However, God does not let you have this feeling of ecstacy unless you have done your best to prepare the best for His glory!

It would be well to review and implement the following steps when preparing your sermons:

1. Be open to the Holy Spirit as you observe the needs of your people. Think of your people as you read the Scriptures. The Holy Spirit will impress upon your heart exactly what they need to hear.

2. Read as many Scripture verses as possible concerning the subject or subjects you are impressed to study and address. Study the clearest and best verses which will support the subject.

3. On a large piece of paper, write down the main Scripture verses, then jot down every conceivable thought which touches the subject. These thoughts come from your heart and experiences, but most importantly, they are impressions from the Holy Spirit. Add to these thoughts the best thoughts you have gleaned from resource books. After following this process, I usually have six or seven pages of raw data when I finish studying.

4. Underline the most exciting and pertinent thoughts on your raw data sheets.

5. Isolate three or four major themes out of the raw data.

6. On separate pieces of paper, write the major themes in sequence. Use one sheet of paper for each theme you write down.

7. Begin to place vital truths and flashes of insight under each major theme from raw data; add new inspirations as they come to you.

8. Arrange these vital truths in logical sequence under each major theme until the entire outline flows with continuity.

9. Flesh these truths out by writing your message, following the outline you have established. Continue to imagine you are speaking to an invisible person who does not know anything about the subject.

10. Prayerfully review your sermon several times. Expect the Holy Spirit to anoint you as you preach.

Chapter 11

Observing Biblical Ordinances

The ordinances of water baptism and Communion are only as meaningful to your people as they are to you. The pastor needs to be comfortable with the mechanics of administering the ordinances so he can effectively minister through them.

To do this he must become acquainted with procedures and be aware of subtle details which often are the reasons the ordinances become a means for embarrassment instead of blessing.

The Ordinance of Water Baptism: Pre-baptism Orientation

Prior to every water baptism, I arrange to meet with those who are going to be baptized. During the orientation you need to cover three main areas with the candidates. First you should *cover the purpose for water baptism.* Hopefully, through discipleship classes or your own teaching, the candidates have received some of the meaning and reason for water baptism.

A brief statement concerning the purpose of baptism can be given to the candidate in the following manner.

"You are about to follow the Lord in baptism. This is a very important event in your Christian life and I want you to understand why it should be one of the most meaningful events in your life.

"You are being baptized first of all because our Lord commanded all of His followers to do so. That in itself is enough to make us want to be baptized. The command has a very important reason. The real meaning behind baptism is identification. You have already been baptized (or identified) by the Spirit into the spiritual body of Christ at the time of your salvation. However, you need to express that spiritual identification in the body of Christ through a local church. In other words, you need to physically identify yourself with Jesus Christ before men and women.

"Baptism is simply a statement to believers and to the world of unbelievers. You are telling others that you have died to the world and sin; you are now identified with Christ and His kingdom.

"The Scriptures tell us that Israel was 'baptized unto Moses' when they crossed the Red Sea. The only people immersed on that day, however, were the Egyptians. The people of Israel were baptized unto Moses only in the sense that they turned their back on Egypt and its slavery and chose to be identified with Moses from that time forward.

"As a believer, when going down into the water, you are

*stating that your old life of sin and slavery to the devil is
gone. It is buried. When you come up out of the water you
are saying that you are now alive in Christ through a new
birth, that you have chosen to be identified with Jesus and
to walk with Him in newness of life. "*

Of course, as pastor you will want to enlarge upon these
statements in your own way. You must remember that it is very
important for those you baptize to be clear about the purpose for
their baptism.

Early in my ministry I learned to ask each candidate to fill out
an information card prior to his/her baptismal service. Upon this
card was written the person's name, the time and place of his/her
conversion, and any significant notations about his/her conversion. Filling out this card makes the candidate pinpoint his/her
salvation and clarify his/her salvation in your mind. I have found
some wanting to be baptized have never had a real conversion
experience.

This card also helps you remember names. Many times in a
ceremonial setting your mind can go blank. You can have a hard
time remembering your own name, let alone others! By having
a time and place of conversion on the cards, you can also give the
confession of faith for people who are extremely nervous or for
those who have a tendency to be unwise or crude with their
remarks.

After your remarks concerning the reason for water baptism,
you will then give the candidates a list of things they will need
to personally prepare for their baptism. These things will include
a complete change of clothes, a bath towel, a man's handkerchief,
a comb, and other items they will need for hair care. Instruct the
candidates to bring all of these items to the church no later than
half an hour prior to the baptismal service.

After going through this list of items with the candidates, you are now ready to have a practice--a *dry* run. Here is what you can say to the candidates.

"When you come into the water, it may feel cold at first. Your first reaction might be to giggle nervously. Do not laugh or joke while you are waiting or when you enter the baptismal tank. This is a serious moment and we must not spoil it. Hand me your card and handkerchief when you come into the tank. I will read from your card. I may ask you to respond, so be prepared to respond to my questions. They will be leading questions so you will not have to worry about what you will say.

"I will put your handkerchief in my right hand to cover your nose and mouth. I will ask you to turn at a right angle in front of me. Don't worry, I will guide you. Then firmly grip my right wrist with both your hands. Your right hand should be on top and your left hand on the bottom of my wrist. Your grip should be fairly firm, but leave your shoulders and elbows relaxed.

"I will say the baptismal formula. Don't anticipate me! Don't try to help me! Don't fight me! You will help by allowing me to take the initiative."

Have several candidates come up and take your wrist and practice flexing their arms properly. This will give them a feeling of confidence about what will happen. Conclude the orientation session with a word of prayer.

Your Own Pre-baptism Preparation

Have those preparing the baptismal tank prepare the water well in advance. The water should be as warm as possible without being hot. You should have the tank filled with as much water as possible without risking spillage when you immerse your candidate. A lot of water gives you leverage and buoyancy to handle the candidates more easily.

Have a person greet and assist the candidates upon their arrival at the church. A lady should be present to assist the women; a man should assist the men. Have your attendants and mop-up crew stay with the candidates. When they are ready to line up for the actual baptism, have your attendants caution all present to be very quiet and reverent.

Hopefully, your church will have baptismal robes available. If baptismal robes are not available, perhaps some of the women could make them. Robes can be inexpensively made from plain white terry cloth or another type of appropriate material. The hems of the robes should be weighted. If making robes is not possible, candidates should wear white clothing which does not become sheer when wet.

There are many appropriate types of baptismal garb for you, the minister. Over the years, I have chosen to wear old slacks, an old white dress shirt, and a bow tie. Other pastors prefer waders and slickers. Your attire for the baptismal service is up to you. Some churches now have tanks where the minister does not even have to get in the water.

When it is time for the service, go into the tank and make a brief statement to your people about the meaning and purpose of baptism. Have prayer for those being baptized. These preliminary remarks and prayer help your congregation feel part of this meaningful service.

When the prayer is finished, signal for the first candidate. Read the candidate's card and give any personal remarks you choose to make. If the candidate has had an unusual conversion, you might want to ask that person to give a brief testimony of his/her experience. Move the candidate in place and have him/her grip your wrist.

My formula for baptism is very simple: *"John Doe, upon the confession of your faith and your determination to live for Jesus Christ all the rest of your days, I do now baptize you in the name of the Father, and of the Son, and of the Holy Spirit."*

It is the actual point of immersion most novices dread. But I believe you will find it is surprisingly easy. The secret is balance and leverage. I am comparatively short, but I have baptized men who were 6'8" with ease. With people over 6 feet tall, I have to be well behind them, reaching up when I give the formula for baptism.

After covering the nose and mouth of the candidate with their handkerchief, gently put the candidate into the water while shifting your own body for good leverage. Lift them up easily by the back of their head and follow them up. You want to be almost directly over the person's head when he/she is submerged. This allows you to get under the head and lift. The buoyancy of the water helps the body to follow easily.

If you are a novice and have a candidate who is disabled or extremely large, it might be wise to enlist help from one of your men in lifting that individual out of the water.

I am very cautious about baptizing very young children unless they show unusual maturity. I encourage special classes on water baptism be taught at the fourth grade level. These classes are part of our regular Sunday school curriculum. I believe that the fourth grade is the proper age when young Christians begin to fully understand why they should follow Christ's example in water baptism.

The baptismal service should end with a song of praise by the congregation. While the congregation is singing, you should take that time to move out of the tank and change your clothes.

Whoever is left in charge of the service can move right along without interruption while you change and prepare to slip into the service for ministry.

The ordinance of water baptism is also a powerful tool of evangelism and witness. Some of my candidates have sent printed invitations to their friends and relatives. Some of those friends and relatives have been unsaved. Through this service, many have been drawn to Christ.

I have baptized hundreds of people during my years of pastoral ministry, and still find water baptism a very meaningful pastoral privilege.

The Communion Service

Once a month, usually the first Sunday morning of the month in most Assemblies of God churches, the ordinance of Communion is administered. The directions in this manual are for the basic month-to-month service.

Methods for observing the ordinance of Communion may vary from church to church, or from pastor to pastor. An entire service may be built around serving Communion, or the Communion service may simply be in addition to the service which the Lord has directed the pastor to hold. The young pastor should, however, learn how to administer a standard Communion service before attempting variations and creative applications.

Pre-service Preparation

Although many things can be done when serving Communion, the success and ease of administering a Communion service is due to careful and prayerful preparations made prior to the service. Your Communion Committee is the key to this. In small churches, one person can prepare the elements easily. Therefore, your "committee" might be one faithful person who looks upon the preparation and clean-up for Communion as a labor of love.

In a large church, this preparation may take the work of several people. It is important to notify your committee at least two days in advance. You need to do this even if your routine day for observing Communion is the first Sunday of the month. Notification will remind them of the preparations needed to be done, and you can use this time to encourage the committee and express your appreciation for their good work and your confidence in them.

Prior to the service, the committee prepares the trays of elements and places them on the Communion table. A clean white cloth is always appropriate to cover the table. Many pastors also like to cover the trays of elements with white cloths.

Communion Servers

In my opinion, how your men and women who serve the elements look and act during the service has a great deal to do with the meaning of the service. Before your service begins, ask those who will serve Communion to meet with you. They may have served Communion for many years, but you need to know what is going to happen on Communion Sunday. It is best to make a practice run through the entire Communion service with those serving.

When you meet with them, first express appreciation for their willingness to serve. Tell them you want to go through a brief rehearsal so everyone will know what will happen--especially yourself. Share with them some of your feelings about the sacredness of Communion. Let them know why you want it to be well done, so that the service will glorify God.

Encourage them to wear the darkest color of suit or dress they own. This manner of dress helps to relate the solemnity and sacredness of the occasion to your congregation.

Tell the servers what your signal will be to begin that part of the service. Usually I will say, "I am asking those who will assist me with Communion to prepare to serve us while we sing." I think it is best for those serving to walk down the center aisle together and stand facing you at the Communion table.

Prior to the serving of the congregation, you might say, *"We are now preparing our hearts for Communion. This ordinance of the church was instituted by our Lord to remember His death. The reason He wanted us to remember Calvary is because it is there we find forgiveness and cleansing from our sin. This is not a closed Communion. Anyone who professes Christ as Savior and Lord, and is depending upon Him alone for their salvation, is encouraged to join us.*

"Please hold both elements in your hands until all are served so we can partake together as a united body of believers. Brother or Sister ---- will lead us in singing while we are being served."

Hand each server a tray of the wine and the bread. When everyone has been given the elements to serve, nod to them as a signal to go to their places and serve the congregation. When everyone has been served, I ask the servers to meet in the lobby of the church and walk back down to the front together. One or two of the servers should be designated to serve the musicians.

When the servers are again facing you, take a tray of each element and serve them. When you have done so, nod as a signal for them to be seated on the front row.

After the servers are seated and the music is finished, it is time for the reading of the Scriptures. I use different passages at different times, but I use the Gospel's account most often. I also use the passage in 1 Corinthians 11, or the first portion of Isaiah

53. After reading the verses, I briefly explain the meaning of each of the elements, encouraging the people to look beyond the symbols to the Savior. This is a time you should allow the Spirit of God to speak through you concerning the finished work of Christ.

After a brief exhortation, pray over the bread, asking God to build faith among your people in His ability to bring wholeness to the total person. Then lift the element and say, *"This is my body which was broken for you. Eat ye all of it."* Then pray over the wine, asking God to build faith among your people in His ability to cleanse us and make us righteous through Calvary's power.

When I am finished, I usually ask the congregation to stand together and sing a verse or two of *Amazing Grace* or another appropriate song as the servers find their places in the congregation and I move to the platform to prepare to preach.

Once in a while I preach on a theme which lends itself to Communion. When I do this, I use the Communion service as the focal point and end the service with Communion.

Most of the time, however, I have Communion prior to preaching, abbreviating the song service and announcements. This gives me greater liberty in what I can preach and allows me to have altar calls to end the service. You will find it is difficult and often repetitious to build a message around Communion every month. I place Communion in the service where I feel it would best minister to the people.

Remember to always inform your servers as to the time when Communion will be served during the service so they will be ready when you call for them.

Make certain you have a pick-up and clean-up committee. Immediate care of your Communion cups prevents breakage and loss.

I use Good Friday night and New Year's Eve services as

substitutes for two of my morning Communion services. This allows children's workers to be involved in a Communion service.

Sometimes I am asked to administer Communion to the sick. I have a portable Communion case which I use on these occasions. I prepare the elements, read the Scriptures, have prayer over each of the elements, and serve the patient or shut-in. This is a very lovely and beautiful part of pastoral ministry.

I have witnessed some special moves of God during Communion services. Since the Lord has commanded us to faithfully administer this ordinance, we can certainly expect His blessing upon it.

Chapter 12

Conducting Weddings: Premarital Counseling and Preparations

One of the most interesting and important parts of pastoral ministry is officiating at weddings. To perform this task with ease and skill takes a great deal of preparation.

The limitations of a manual of this size make it impossible to anticipate all the variations, personalities, and surprises. However, it is my goal to provide adequate coaching to cover most contingencies.

Premarital Counseling

This subject fills many fine volumes. To learn as much about the subject as possible, I suggest that you read several books about the subject which have been written by evangelical writers. The magnitude of the subject is intimidating to the new pastor until he learns that his role in all pastoral counseling is compassionate listening and the giving of godly advice based upon the dynamics of biblical truths. The role of a pastor in premarital counseling is not to be a psychologist. A pastor's role is that of a concerned friend trying to smooth the marital road.

Premarital counseling can become a very detailed and extensive program in your church. At the time of the writing of this manual, my former church requires all couples wishing to be married by any of our ministers to complete a 13-week course on marriage. This course is taught by a competent, licensed counselor. Several videocassettes of my own teachings are also used during these sessions.

In most instances, you will probably know the couple quite well. However, there are times when you will not know one or possibly both of the people who want to be married. It is when you do not know the couple that you must determine whether you will marry them. I say, "I do not know your fiance well, so you won't mind my asking a few questions I am sure. First of all, is he/she a believer?" If the fiance is not a believer, I refuse to marry a believer to an unbeliever on scriptural grounds.

Then I say, "Is this the first marriage." If there is a divorce in the background, I say, "I will have to talk with you both before I can determine whether I can perform the ceremony."

Where divorce has taken place, I face the problem openly. To the best of my ability I ascertain whether I can marry the couple or not upon what I determine as scriptural grounds. I turn down about half the requests I receive for second and third marriages.

If I cannot marry them, I tell them diplomatically but firmly, "I am sure you will be disappointed when I tell you I cannot officiate at your ceremony in good conscience. You will have to understand this is not anything to do with you personally. If it were my own daughter, I could not do it because I do not believe you have scriptural grounds for remarriage. You can choose to be angry with me, but I trust you will understand why I cannot marry you. I would further encourage you to prayerfully reconsider your marriage plans." [*Who ever said pastoring is easy?*]

When you must do all the counseling by yourself, it is necessary to cover the most vital areas of marriage in one or two sessions. The best you can do for extensive counseling with limited staff and resources is to recommend the couple read a book or two together.

I suggest you read several books on Christian marriage so you can personally recommend books to them. It would be wise to recommend books in paperback so you can stock three or four copies at the church. This assures you the couple has the material in hand.

If money is tight in your church budget, charge the couple for the books at the church's cost.

There are several areas which you need to cover in counseling couples. The first thing I do after making the decision as to whether I will marry the couple or not is to review the details of the wedding with them. This includes the date of the wedding, the rehearsal date and dinner, and the reception.

I ask them what functions they wish for me to attend and if they expect me to participate in any way. I have learned to do this because there have been occasions when I was uncertain whether my wife and I were expected to be at a rehearsal dinner. There have also been times when I have learned that I was expected to emcee a reception and had not been given any advance notice.

After taking care of these peripheral activities, I move quickly to the wedding itself.

First, establish whether they want the traditional wedding

ceremony. If they want another ceremony, make note of it. If it is one you do not have, ask them to type a copy for you. This should be typed on paper which will fit into the marriage handbook you use during these ceremonies.

Ask the couple to bring the ceremony to you at least a week prior to the wedding so you will have time to read and approve it. I always maintain the right to include or edit material. The wedding arrangements are at the will of the bride, but the ceremony itself is subject to my own convictions.

After establishing the basic wedding ceremony, ask them to go through the wedding step by step. Most of the time they will not be able to do so; thus, you should help them. Give the bride a piece of paper and ask that she write down the order of the service while you make notes on the wedding yourself.

Here are questions which must be answered:

> *How many songs will you have during the wedding ceremony?* This question should be asked first so you can space the music properly.

> *When the men come in with me, will the groom and best man go down to meet you at the aisle?*

> *Will your father give you away? Will you want a song at that time?*

> *Do you want me to make any informal remarks or go right into the ceremony?*

> *Do you want Communion served to the bride and groom?* [This is another good place for a song.]

> *Do you want to kiss the bride?*

> *Will you have a unity candle?* [The lighting of this candle is another good place for a song.]

> *Do you want me to announce the reception following the ceremony?*

If the bride does not have the answers to these questions, ask her to get you the information as quickly as possible.

When you have settled basic questions about the wedding, it is time to move to actual counseling. I use the following method.

"Now that we have covered some of the details of the wedding, I would like to go over some very important things. After every wedding there is a marriage. That marriage is what I am concerned about. I am not a psychologist, but the Bible has a lot to say about marriage and I have discovered some important principles.

"The first problem most young couples encounter is financial. One of you should take care of the checkbook so there is no confusion about who pays the bills on time. Provide enough petty cash for each one's needs once a week. If you spend more than the petty cash agreed upon, be sure to talk it over. This constant checking about money is not to be judgmental, only informational. You should have a plan for your money or you will not control your money.

"Well established counselors have determined that the 70-20-10 plan is practical. After your tithes and taxes are taken out of your paycheck, 70 percent should go for housing and living expenses. No more than 20 percent should go for time payments--other than your house-- including car, furniture, appliances, and all other needs.

"Ten percent should go into a savings account. You should try to give yourself a 10 percent cut to put into savings from the very beginning. Although it might be hard, if you don't start saving while your income is small, you won't save when your income grows.

"The second area I want to cover is in-laws. The first rule is not to ever live with them. The second rule is that you

are responsible for each of your parents. If there should be a problem, he is responsible to deal with his; she is responsible to deal with hers. If the groom's mother begins to tell the bride what to do, it is the groom's duty to tell his mother to ease up.

"A lot of marriages break up because one in the marriage does not leave father and mother and cleave to his/her spouse. You continue to love and honor your parents, but they do not have any control over your lives anymore.

"Determine now how many holidays you are going to spend with each set of in-laws. Be very sensitive to spending too much time with your parents and diplomatically control how often your parents come to visit you. They are your parents, but they are not your partner's parents, as wonderful as they may be. Don't always ask your partner to go with you to visit your parents if you see them often.

"The next area I want to discuss with you is sex. Sex is a wonderful part of your relationship and you need to be prepared for it within Christian guidelines.

"Most young couples want to know what is considered a normal sex life. Normal is what is comfortable and enjoyable for both partners. I have known young couples who enjoyed having sex every night and others who were more comfortable having sex once a week or every 10 days.

"You should not have children for at least a year after your wedding. This gives you an opportunity for adjustment to marriage and your partner.

"This statement brings us to the topic of birth control. The Bible says nothing definitive about birth control. This means you are allowed your own discretion. The bride should visit her doctor and seek advice about which birth

control method should be used.

"The Bible says: The marriage bed is undefiled. Therefore, there should be no sense of guilt about sex in marriage. Keep it meaningful and beautiful. Remember also that the woman has different sexual needs. Become sensitive to her monthly period and be considerate of the physiological changes in her body during this time. Always keep your bodies clean for each other. If you run into sex problems, be sure to seek out a good Christian counselor. There is no need for you to be frustrated in this area."

At this point I begin to give the couple some general attitudes about their individual roles in their marriage. I begin by saying,

"The Bible says the husband is to be head of the home while loving his wife as Christ loved the church. This does not mean the husband is better, it simply means the husband's role is different from the wife's and vice versa.

"When you have discussions, both should communicate opinions, feelings, and judgments without anger. Always maintain an attitude of trying to do what is best to strengthen the relationship. When you have both honestly communicated your feelings, it is the husband's duty to make the final decision.

"I always have contended that when people are truly in love there is wholesome communication whether they say anything or not. Have the will and desire to understand each other. Constantly try to put yourself in your partner's situation. Don't be threatened by differences; learn to appreciate them. Remember, marriage doesn't change people, it simply reveals more of what they really are. Love will change your partner 10 times faster than anything else.

"Keep your marriage strong by building confidence in

each other. Do things together. Turn off the television and talk. Read a book together and discuss it. Surprise each other with special acts of love. Compliment each other. Encourage each other. Make sure you stay the best of friends."

When I know the couple understands the things I have said, I then explain that I want to talk with them about the most important thing in their marriage: their relationship with God. I say,

"Right from the start I want you to promise me something! On your honeymoon and every day after, I want you to read the Bible together and pray for God's blessing upon your lives and activities for that day. Will you promise me now you will do that? Learn to talk about spiritual things with ease. Encourage each other in your Christian walk."

Many young couples seem to have difficulty being faithful to the church when they are first married. This is a tragedy because the church can give them spiritual strength and help them develop wholesome relationships. Knowing this, I urge the couple to be active and faithful to the church from the very beginning. I let them know that the church doesn't need them half as much as they need the church. I encourage them to support the church with their tithes, explaining that when they honor God, He will honor them.

I explain to them that unsaved friends can have a tremendous influence on them and that through the church they will be able to find the kind of friends they need. I let the couple know that it is perfectly right to minister to the unsaved, to love them and pray for them. Yet I point out that when these unsaved people begin to affect them spiritually, they must back away from them. I always remind them that while their human relationships may last a lifetime, their relationship with God will last forever.

I ask the couple if there are any real spiritual differences or questions concerning the doctrines of the church. After responding to these questions, I ask if they have any questions concerning anything I have said, anything I need to clarify. Most of the time the couple will not have many questions.

If the couple surfaces some real problems, you will need to set up another session just to talk with them about those needs in detail.

At this point you should remind them about the necessary legal documents and blood tests. Explain that they must go to the office of the county clerk and pick up their marriage license and certificate. Tell them to type in the information required, and bring these documents to the wedding rehearsal.

You must have both documents signed after the wedding. Give the best man the marriage certificate. Have the best man present the certificate to the bride and groom after the wedding or reception as proof of marriage. Send in the marriage license to the state yourself.

Perhaps there are special circumstances surrounding the marriage. Pre-marital counseling is a real opportunity to minister. Take it seriously. Pray about each case. You must have the anointing of the Spirit to give wise counsel.

Go into each session genuinely interested in helping the couple. With the Lord's help and your concern, you will make a lifelong impact upon those you counsel.

Close all your pre-marital counseling sessions with prayer.

I suggest you read over this chapter several times, then add your own experiences and observations as your ministry progresses.

Chapter 13

Conducting Weddings:
The Wedding Rehearsal,
the Wedding,
and the Reception

The key to a beautiful wedding is not how much money is spent; the key to a beautiful wedding is found in how much care is taken to details prior to the ceremony.

I have been to weddings where the church was beautifully decorated, the music exquisite, the wedding party elegantly dressed--yet the wedding resembled a nervous circus. Why? Because people were not clear what was to be done, nor were they clear about who was supposed to do what needed to be done!

To orchestrate a smooth-running wedding is truly an art. The pastor should develop competent wedding consultants in his church to assist in making the arrangements, running the rehearsal, and supervising the wedding itself. However, until such assistants are found and trained, the minister must know all the details--as well as how to handle each of them--in order to assure couples meaningful wedding ceremonies. Even if the pastor has a capable person trained in wedding etiquette, he must still know everything about a wedding in order to lend support to consultants when they are fulfilling their role or to give direction when unusual questions or requests come to him.

The directions I am going to give to those reading this manual are long and detailed. However, they are very necessary if you wish to avoid confusion.

Before addressing the mechanics of the wedding, it is necessary to remember some basic philosophies.

First of all, remember that the wedding you conduct is a Christian ceremony with strong overtones of worship. It is your responsibility to keep the service and activities surrounding the service within guidelines which do not violate your Christian convictions.

For instance, I do not allow any form of alcoholic beverages on the church grounds. I insist on the wedding party being sober at the rehearsal and the wedding. I also insist on the right to overrule any objectionable music.

Second, since you are officiating, you reserve the right to include what you feel is necessary in a Christian ceremony or to deny requests which would make you uncomfortable. For instance, I tried conducting a wedding once where my back was to the audience with the bride and groom facing the audience. I will never do that again because the attention of the bridal party was not on the ceremony; their attention was on the audience.

Third, within the boundaries of Christian conduct, basic etiquette, and church rules, the bride should have the type of wedding she wants. It is *her* wedding. This should be made clear to everyone (including the bride's mother) in a nice but firm way.

Fourth, build systems which nail down all details before

rehearsal time. The rehearsal is not for the purpose of deciding how the wedding will be run, it is a time for implementing the decisions which have already been made.

Pre-rehearsal Conference

Approximately 90 days before the wedding, you or your consultant should meet with the bride and groom. If desired, the bride's mother may also attend this session. This meeting is to help them see the decisions which need to be made and help you determine what special arrangements you might need to make.

When they come to your office, have prayer with them. Ask God to bless all of the arrangements. Give each one a *Wedding Personnel Form*. A sample copy of this form follows.

Wedding Personnel Form

Bride's Legal Name _____ Phone _____

Date of Wedding _____ Date of Rehearsal _____

ATTENDANTS:

   Maid or Matron of Honor _____

   Bridesmaids _____

   _____

   _____

   _____

   Flower Girl _____

Groom's Legal Name _____

   Best Man _____

   Groomsmen _____

   _____

   _____

   _____

   Ring Bearer _____

   Ushers _____

   _____

Guest Book Attendant _____

Candle Lighters _____

Who is Giving Bride Away _____

Organist _____ Pianist _____

Soloist _____

Music _____

_____

_____

Reserved Seating for Family - Approximate Number:

Bride _____ Groom _____

Florist - (Staples are not allowed on church furniture) _____

_____

Photographer _____

Sound Man _____

Video Man _____

Printer _____

Caterer _____

Equipment Needed _____

_____

_____

After tailoring this form to fit your personal needs, have a supply printed and kept in the church files.

One person, usually the bride, fills out the form. You should fill out your copy as she fills out hers. You will keep your copy for your records.

If they cannot complete the form that day, ask that they call you with the rest of the information as soon as possible so you can complete your records.

After the *Wedding Personnel Form* is completed you are ready to fill out the *Wedding Program Form*. This form is vital for both the bride and yourself. Fill this form out together. If all of the information is not available, instruct the bride to call you with the information as soon as it is finalized. A copy of the form I have used follows.

Wedding Program Form

Ceremony to Giving Bride Away _____
   Song (if desired) _____
Ceremony _____
Pronounce Man and Wife; Kneel for (Communion) and Prayer

_____
   Song (if desired) _____
Unity Candles? _____
   Song (if desired) _____
Pastoral Greeting _____
Groom Kisses Bride _____
Recessional
Pastoral Announcement and Dismissal _____
Usher Bride's Parents Out _____
Usher Groom's Parents Out _____

It is all right to offer names of business establishments and wedding services if they ask. Make certain the firms you recommend are reputable. It is good to have an official church florist. However, though you can recommend that florist, it is wise to say, "I have heard good reports about these people but you will have to decide who you want to use."

Instruct the bride to notify the musicians as early as possible to arrange a special rehearsal. The wedding rehearsal is not a music rehearsal. Tell the bride to inform the musicians that they will be needed at the wedding rehearsal only for the purpose of learning the procedures. The musicians should have practiced their music prior to the wedding rehearsal.

You will notice on the *Wedding Program Form* that I have provided several places where songs would be appropriate. Few brides want four or five songs during the ceremony. Normally two or three songs are used.

Several days before the rehearsal it would be wise to contact the bride or her official representative to see if there are any last minute changes. Remind the bride at that time that she is responsible for the wedding party being at the rehearsal on time. The personnel who should attend the rehearsal includes all attendants, the parents, and the musicians.

The church platform should be cleared prior to the rehearsal. Men attendants could be asked to come a few minutes early to clear the platform and set it up for the wedding if you do not have a custodian available to handle this.

The Rehearsal and the Wedding

At the announced time for the rehearsal, call for everyone involved in the wedding to gather in a group at the front of the church. Introduce yourself and then say, "We want to welcome you to the wedding rehearsal for ------ and ------. We all want this wedding to be the most meaningful time in their lives. I am going to ask you to pray with me that the rehearsal and wedding will not be just a routine ritual, but a time of Christian worship and sharing. Let us pray."

After prayer, the first order of business is to place the wedding party on the platform just as they will stand in the ceremony. When everyone is in place, ask someone to mark each place the people are to stand with a small piece of tape. Places for the bride, the groom, or yourself will not be marked.

With everyone in place, say, "In a moment we will run through the entire wedding ceremony. During the entire program I want you to look as happy and relaxed as possible. I do not need to remind you, however, this is a sacred service. I want everyone to maintain good decorum and behavior throughout the proceedings."

It is at this point you will go through the wedding program with them to give them an idea of what is going to happen.

There are many things which you should know concerning what should happen on the wedding day. One important thing is knowing when the wedding party should arrive at the church. If everyone is to be dressed for the wedding prior to coming to the church, all of the wedding party should be at the church 30 minutes before the wedding.

A Bride's Room should be designated in the church and used for all weddings. The room should be large enough for the bride and her attendants to prepare themselves. The room should have mirrors, if possible. A bathroom, to be used by the bride and attendants, should be located close to the bride's room.

The groom and groomsmen should also have a designated room to meet and prepare themselves. If the wedding party plans to dress at the church, they should come early enough to insure that everyone is ready for the wedding 30 minutes prior to the announced time.

Thirty minutes prior to the announced wedding time, ushers take their stations with printed programs in hand (if applicable). After handing programs to the guests, ushers offer their right or left arm (depending upon which side of the aisle she will be seated) to the lady. The lady's escort and/or children follow behind. When a single man presents himself, I prefer an usher lead him to a seat. Etiquette, however, permits the usher to simply point to the area where the man should sit.

I strongly recommend that children under the age of 5 be met by an adult who will take them to the back or side of the church to be supervised during the wedding. The reason for this precaution is obvious. Small children are delightful; however, I have seen them destroy the sacredness of the wedding service.

The wedding party should be dressed and in their designated

areas 30 minutes prior to the beginning of the ceremony. The photographer should use this time to take candid shots of the wedding party in each area.

The person in charge of the guest book is also in place 30 minutes prior to the ceremony.

The sanctuary should be cleared of all activity. Decorations are completed, microphones set, and all pre-wedding photographs in the sanctuary taken by this time. Should guests arrive 30 minutes before the wedding is to begin, they should see a sanctuary ready. There should be no one moving about, preparing last-minute details.

The pastor has the responsibility of taking care of Communion elements at this time if Communion is to be observed.

Twenty minutes prior to the wedding the prelude should begin. If the bride is going to have the candles pre-lit (no visible candle lighters), have two of the ushers or other designated personnel light them. Request that the bride use no-drip candles. You might also request that squares of plasti-glass be placed under each candelabra to protect the floor.

If a white aisle cloth is to be used, two of the ushers should roll the cloth into place about 5 minutes prior to the ceremony. Many are discouraging the use of an aisle cloth because a cloth on top of carpeting often causes ladies wearing high heels to trip.

The most important thing to remember is: *Start the wedding on time!*

If candlelighters are used, the cue for the wedding begins with them coming down the side aisle together. They may stay at the front or return to the back of the church by exiting down the center aisle together. This is at the discretion of the bride.

If candles are pre-lit, the cue for the wedding to begin is the ushering of the groom's grandparents to their seats. The bride's grandparents follow the groom's. Two ushers should be designated as special ushers. One will take care of seating the groom's parents, the other takes care of seating the bride's mother. They will also escort the parents out of the sanctuary.

After the grandparents are seated, the groom's parents are seated. This is followed by the seating of the bride's mother.

If any of the ushers who seat the parents are going to serve as groomsmen, the moment they are finished seating the parents they should move quickly to join the minister and the rest of the men because the men will come out almost immediately after the parents are seated.

If all ushers serve as groomsmen, a person should be appointed to assist latecomers. The person appointed would not need to be dressed in formal attire.

After the parents are seated, many brides desire to have a song sung. Remember, at the rehearsal have soloists sing only one or two lines of each song--just enough to give the wedding party a feel for what will be happening.

A prearranged song should serve as a cue for the minister to lead the groom, best man, and groomsmen to their places. The men should walk to the front about an arm's length apart in a dignified manner. A diagram of the placement of the men prior to the bride's appearance follows.

The minister and all the men should look toward the back of the church where the bridesmaids will appear.

After the men are in place, it is time for the bridesmaids to begin their processional. They should walk, one at a time, down the aisle in a stately, unhurried manner. The bride or the pastor should appoint someone to assist the ladies while they are getting ready for the ceremony. This person will also serve as coordinator for the ladies and be responsible for giving cues to the bridesmaids and bride as to when they should enter the sanctuary. It is wise to have this coordinator also attend the rehearsal.

As each bridesmaid approaches the front, her corresponding groomsman serves as her escort and offers his arm to her. If they must go up steps, he should take her by the elbow and assist her. The last bridesmaid is followed by the maid or matron of honor.

If there are to be a flower girl and ring bearer, they should come after the maid of honor. The flower girl is the maid of honor's responsibility and the ring bearer is in the charge of the best man.

If the rings are on the ring bearer's pillow, the maid of honor should remove the groom's ring and the best man should take the bride's ring at this time.

The bride is now ready to make her appearance on the right arm of her escort. The bride's mother should be instructed to stand when the bride appears at the open door and begins her walk down the aisle to the altar. This is the cue for all wedding guests to stand. The bride, with her escort, comes to the front. The groom moves toward the bride, and together they wait for you to begin the ceremony.

When all are in their places, your first words are, "You may be seated." When the guests are seated, you may begin the formal part of the ceremony. It has become a tradition 90 percent of the time for me to give a brief informal pastoral homily of about 5 to 7 minutes before I begin reading the wedding ceremony. I often bring in practical aspects of marriage and personal influences to the couple if I know them well.

Following this brief homily, I begin to read the ceremony. I continue reading to the point where it says, "Who giveth this woman to be married to this man?" The escort usually responds by saying, "Her mother and I." If the bride's mother is not present, he says, "I do." If the escort is the father of the bride, it is appropriate for him to kiss the bride and then take her hand and place it in the groom's. He should then sit down next to the bride's mother.

The bride and groom now stand alone. Quite often a song is sung at this point. Near the end of the song the bride and groom move up to the altar. If no song is sung, the bride and groom immediately move up to the altar in front of you as soon as the bride is given away.

When the couple is in front of you, the bride hands her bouquet to her maid of honor. If she forgets to do this, quietly remind her to do so. Instruct the entire wedding party during the rehearsal to turn toward the bride and groom as they move up in front of you. Below are diagrams for placement of the wedding party during this time.

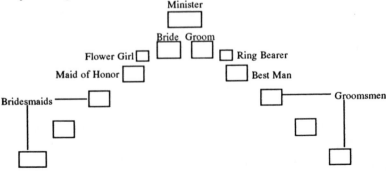

You are now ready to proceed with the wedding ceremony. During the rehearsal you should practice with a couple of substitute rings. The best man should hand the bride's ring to you. The signal for this to happen is when you reach out to the groom with the palm of your hand up. In turn, you give the ring to the groom. The maid of honor will hand the groom's ring to you and you will hand it to the bride.

After the ceremony is complete, pronounce them husband and wife. After that point, invoke God's blessings as they stand before you. If a kneeling bench is available, ask them to kneel during this time. During rehearsal, instruct the groom to assist the bride down and up by taking her arm. She kneels first, he gets up first.

If there is Communion, administer the elements at the proper time. Often there is another appropriate song sung during Communion. I choose to make Communion very personal. I lower my voice and explain to them how Calvary is the place of love and forgiveness. I encourage them to kneel at the Cross when there are difficulties and strain in their relationship. Then I administer the Communion elements. The groom should assist the bride when it is her turn to partake of the cup. After the song is finished and the time for Communion is completed, I pray a pastoral prayer. As you say "Amen," the bride and groom need to stand.

If there is to be a unity candle, the couple should move toward it. At rehearsal those who might block the path of the bride and groom to the unity candle should be instructed to move back to let them through. The couple then lights the center candle with their side candles. The groom should blow out the bride's candle for her because her gown is often a fire hazard. After lighting the candle they should stand in place if a song is sung, then return to stand in front of you. Instruct the maid of honor to assist the bride if the train of her gown needs adjusting.

When they stand before you as husband and wife, you should greet them by saying, "Mr. and Mrs. -----, I wish you much happiness. I congratulate you. God bless you both." Then, raising your voice a bit, say, "You may now kiss your bride."

At the rehearsal I have the bride and groom practice the kiss. I have a bit of fun with it, but they know I am serious. I say, "I want you to practice the kiss. I don't want a love scene, nor do I want you to give her a passing peck. I want you to give the bride a good, solid smack on the lips. Now, give it a try." There are times when I have had to give them instruction two or three times until the kiss is proper.

When the couple has kissed, the maid of honor should hand the bride's bouquet back to her. Have the couple turn, then announce with a loud and happy voice, "Ladies and gentlemen, it is my delightful privilege to introduce to you Mr. and Mrs. ----------."

The recessional should immediately start. The wedding party should be instructed to exit with appropriate spacing. The honor attendants go first. The flower girl and ring bearer should follow the honor attendants out. If the children don't move, the next attendants should help them. I suggest the bridesmaids with their escorts begin to move from the platform as each couple reaches the first row of pews.

As soon as the wedding party has exited, the special ushers should come back to usher out the bride's parents first, then the groom's parents. If grandparents wish to be ushered out, then the ushers should come back and usher out the bride's grandparents first and then the groom's grandparents.

When the parents have been ushered out, you may make any requested announcements. This could be, "Please remain seated until the ushers can assist you. You are invited to attend the reception at ------. Thank you for attending. God bless you."

You may then leave the platform.

The ushers should be instructed to usher people out row by row, starting at the front of the church.

The receiving line should be formed at the reception unless the reception is some distance from the church, or unless not all guests have been invited to attend the reception. There are times, however, when the bride prefers to have the receiving line in the foyer, immediately following the ceremony. This is quite proper. A diagram of the receiving line follows.

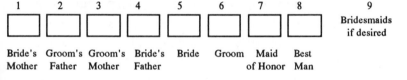

1	2	3	4	5	6	7	8	9
Bride's Mother	Groom's Father	Groom's Mother	Bride's Father	Bride	Groom	Maid of Honor	Best Man	Bridesmaids if desired

You should attend the reception if possible. If you cannot, your apologies and reasons should be given ahead of time. A suggested format for the reception is as follows:

Refreshments should be served to guests upon their arrival.

Upon the arrival of the bride and groom to the reception (which should not be more than 30 minutes following the wedding), the couple should immediately cut the cake and receive a toast from the best man if he is prepared to do so. When the cake is cut, the receiving line should be formed if it has not been done in the foyer of the church.

Following the receiving line, the prepared program (if there is to be one) should be introduced. Following the program is the throwing of the bride's bouquet and garter. Then there is the farewell and clean-up.

Several decisions should be made by the bride well in advance of the wedding in regard to the photographer. As the minister, you should have some basic rules as well. A decision should be made early as to whether the formal pictures will be taken before or after the wedding. If the pictures are taken prior to the wedding, the photographer must be told he or she must be out of the sanctuary 30 minutes prior to the wedding.

If pictures are to be taken after the wedding, inform the photographer the job must be completed within a 30-minute limit after the last guest has been ushered out so as not to keep people waiting too long at the reception.

It is important to instruct the wedding party to go to a designated private room from the recessional if pictures are going to be taken following the wedding in the sanctuary. If you do not do this, the wedding party will mingle with the guests and you will never get them together for photographs.

I have never allowed flash pictures to be taken by any guest or professional photographer during the ceremony. If there is a printed program, I have this rule printed there. Flash pictures are very disruptive.

I have stopped the ceremony on several occasions and said, "Thank you for not taking flash pictures during the ceremony. It is important to the sacredness of the wedding." I do not allow flash pictures even if the bride requests it. You must explain to her that if you allowed it at all, her wedding would become a three-ring circus with everyone bringing their flash cameras.

I allow professional photographers to take time exposure pictures from the back of the church during the ceremony. This does not disturb the ceremony.

Other suggestions I want to give include:

1. Fill out your part of the official documents prior to the wedding. When you leave the platform following the wedding, go to your office and pick up the documents which need to be signed. As soon as you return to the sanctuary, ask the witnesses to sign the papers and give the

signed marriage certificate to the best man. Tell him to give it to the groom when convenient. After pictures which include me are taken, I return the completed Marriage License to my office as soon as possible. Be sure to mail it to the county registrar immediately after the reception or the first thing the next day.

2. Use your own discretion in attending the rehearsal dinner. Most often you will be invited. That dinner does give you a good opportunity to meet new people. If you are going to the reception, however, do not feel obligated to go to the rehearsal dinner. If you plan to go, however, be very clear the groom knows. His parents traditionally pay for this dinner.

3. When meeting with the men prior to going into the wedding, I jokingly ask to look at the bottoms of the groom's shoes. I have been able to avoid unnecessary embarrassment by catching messages painted on the bottom of the shoes for the benefit of the audience to read when the groom kneels for prayer.

4. For special occasions when I use a ceremonial book of any kind, I use blank paper with an applied tear-off glue on one side as my own insert. On this page for weddings, I place the full names of the bride and groom, any cues I need to remember, and a brief order of the service. After the service I simply remove the paper from my book. This way you don't have to write in your manuals.

Chapter 14

Conducting Funerals

It would be wise to study these procedures before you are called to officiate at a funeral. This will allow you to concentrate on sermon preparation when called. You are not usually given much time to prepare for a funeral.

Pre-service Procedures and Details

When you hear of a death in your church, promptly contact an immediate family member and determine where the family is gathering so you can meet with them for prayer. Ask the question, "Would it be convenient for me to come over now to pray with the family?" They will give you some indication of when it would be best for you to meet with them. If a member of the family calls first, it is really a summons to go to the family immediately unless they tell you differently.

Your role on the initial visit is as a minister and resource person. As a minister, you should realize that at this time your greatest ministry is simply being there. The pastor cares and is concerned about the bereaved.

Do not dominate the proceedings. Minister to the family when it is obviously needed, but otherwise be very low key. Don't stay long. Gather everyone together before you leave and pray for God's comfort.

As a resource person you stand ready to help if asked. Before a death occurs in your congregation, become acquainted with at least one funeral director. Call a couple of well-established clergymen in your area and ask them two questions:

1) What funeral home is the most reliable and efficient? and

2) What is the cost of an average funeral in your area?

If the family wants you to help them with funeral arrangements, simply recommend a funeral home and offer to call the funeral director for them. A reputable funeral director will take care of every detail.

Sometimes the family will want you to go to the funeral home and help them with purchasing the casket and making the arrangements. In that case, offer to meet the family at the funeral home with the director.

If the family seems to be comfortable in making their own arrangements or has already made some preparatory arrangements, do not suggest accompanying them to the funeral home.

If you are asked to be with the family when they meet with the director, be careful not to be too aggressive in dictating what should be done. Be part of the family and listen. Do not voice your opinion until asked unless there is something way out of line.

When asked your opinion, say something in this order: "In my opinion we should have a very nice service without being extravagant. Could I suggest choosing a modest but adequate casket?" Your job is to lend support to the family and make certain they are not pressured into a high-priced casket and/or funeral arrangements because of guilt or emotion.

If the burial plot has not been chosen, they may want you to help with this also. Here again, moderation in cost is the key. Some people want a mausoleum. If the family feels strongly about a mausoleum or a high-priced burial plot, don't interfere.

If they decide upon cremation, go along with it unless you have some theological problem with cremation. Personally, I do not have a problem with this. I feel cremation simply speeds up the natural processes.

You may be asked to arrange music for the funeral and to contact pallbearers. Do these as soon as possible, reporting back to both the funeral director and the family.

Most churches have a group of ladies who arrange to prepare funeral dinners for the families. This is a necessary and valid ministry. The dinner is usually at the church or in the home of a family member. While making funeral arrangements, be sure to have a clear understanding as to whether the family wants to have a dinner provided.

If you have a morning funeral, the noon meal would be prepared. If the funeral is in the afternoon, it is usually convenient to have the dinner soon after the burial. Make sure a competent person is in charge to work with the family on the number of people anticipated and to follow through with contacting church people on what foods to bring and when and where they should be brought.

Ask a knowledgeable person in the church what the normal procedures are in sending flowers from the church. If they do not have any, call a couple of board members and ask their opinion on how much should be spent on a floral arrangement. Establish a policy at your official board meeting on flowers for funerals and special occasions. Have the florist send flowers to the funeral home as soon as possible. The card should be signed from you, your spouse, and the church.

If you have a regular church service before the funeral is to occur, announce the time and place of the funeral at that time.

I make it a point to stop by the funeral home a day or two before the service to view the body. I sign the memorial registration book at that time. I also minister through prayer and encouragement to those family members who are viewing the body.

The following is a checklist of things which you should do or know prior to the funeral service:

· Have prayer with the family soon after the death.
· Be available as a resource person.
· Do they want you to arrange any music?
· Do they want you to help obtain pallbearers?
· Do they want a funeral dinner?
· If they want a dinner, who will organize the dinner and contact the family and church members about the time, number, and amount of food needed?
· Are flowers sent from the church?
· Pay your respects at funeral home.

The Funeral Service

Throughout the years I have become very comfortable with the following procedures and order of service. You will want to make adjustments to these suggestions to fit your own personality.

I usually arrive 10 to 15 minutes prior to the announced time of the funeral. Usually the funeral director takes you to a side room to go over the clergyman's record he will give you.

If you have been in touch with the family, all of the information on the clergyman's record will have already been given to you. Pronounce the names of all the surviving members of the family on the record you plan to read. Sometimes I have had to ask the funeral director to find out the proper pronunciation from a member of the family. Write the names phonetically over the printed names so you do not embarrass yourself and others when you read the names.

Often, members of the family want to see you for a few minutes. In some cases, distraught people need prayer. Because you are there early, there is time to slip around and have prayer with people in the family section if you are needed.

The funeral director will take you or show you to your seat near the podium.

Bring three copies of an order of service to the funeral: *one for the director, one for the musicians (if applicable), and one for yourself.*

My order of service usually looks like this:

> *Song* (if requested)
> *Opening remarks*
> *Scripture reading*
> *Poem* (if applicable)
> *Obituary*
> *Prayer*
> *Song* (if requested)
> *Sermon*
> *Prayer*

If the family has asked another minister to take part, simply assign him any part of the service you feel appropriate. If he is an old family friend, he should take the prayer, Scripture reading, and obituary with personal remarks.

If only one song is requested, place it after your first prayer in the order of service.

My opening remarks are only a few sentences. They include why we are gathered, acknowledging the power of faith to overcome the sorrow of hearts. Then I say, "At times like this, it is a privilege to be able to turn to God's Word. I have selected ------." If it was a favorite scriptural passage of the deceased, mention it. Often the family will request a poem. This is included in the order of service.

The obituary is an opportunity to include your own personal remarks and feelings about the deceased. Many times the family has written an obituary for you when you requested information from them in preparing the details of the service. Always maintain control of what is said and who says it. When experiencing deep sorrow and grief, well-intentioned people often want things done, said, or read with which you are not comfortable. Be diplomatic, but always maintain the right to edit information in order to make the service meaningful.

In the obituary I often speak of the last time I visited with the deceased and what was said. Be personal, but do not try to fake a close relationship if it was not there. If you didn't know the deceased well, use family references to the deceased instead of your own.

Read the list of survivors listed on the back of your clergy record. Then say, "Let us join our hearts in prayer for this family and all who are touched by the passing of ------."

After prayer there may be a song. Then it is time for the sermon. The funeral sermon should be 15 to 20 minutes in length, scripturally sound, spiritually appealing, and practically comforting. Speak to the living. Your eulogy of the dead should be done in the obituary.

If the deceased was an unbeliever, speak to the living about Jesus. Don't put the deceased in heaven when you don't have any reason to think the person is in heaven. Challenge the people in the light of death to give their lives to Christ, to invest their lives in something that outlives time, to commit their lives to Christ and His love.

If the deceased was an exemplary believer, refer to him/her in examples and illustrations of his/her life if it strengthens the message.

If you will remember the funeral sermon is a message to the living and not a eulogy to the dead, this will free you to deliver a Christ-centered message--even if the deceased was an unbeliever or a suicide.

After the message, pray and sit down. The funeral director will then usher the people around the casket. When the last of the audience and the pallbearers pass by the casket, get up and pay your respects. Then you should move to the head of the casket and prepare to assist the family.

Most families keep good control. Once in a while, however, there is extreme behavior. Most often you will find that the funeral director is trained to handle extreme behavior. You simply assist him. If the funeral director does nothing, quietly talk with the distraught person and have members of the family help you take the person out.

Once in a while a person might faint. Don't expect this because it is rare, but be prepared for it when it happens by remaining very calm. Assure the family it will be all right. The funeral director invariably has smelling salts. Assist in any way you can without becoming upset yourself.

If there is not a committal service, the funeral director and his staff will take care of the body. You move out with the family, thanking the funeral director before you leave.

If there is a committal service, stay with the body while the funeral staff prepares the casket for transport to the grave. Lead the way a few feet ahead of the casket to the hearse. Step aside so the pallbearers can place the casket in the hearse.

If the burial is nearby, I ride in the hearse. This gives me opportunity to get better acquainted with the staff, and, also, I do not have to worry about driving in the procession or parking. If it is necessary to take my car, I have the attendant tag it before I go into the funeral and then follow the processional wherever the director places me.

When you arrive at the place of burial, move to the rear of the hearse and prepare to lead the processional to the grave. If the casket is to be carried any distance, ask the funeral director what path would be best to take. Stay about 6 feet ahead of the processional, glancing over your shoulder to keep a proper gait and distance.

Stand at the head of the casket until the family is seated and the pall bearers placed. The funeral director will nod to you when it is time to begin the committal service.

The committal service should be very brief. If the deceased was a believer, I often refer to Paul's analogy of the seed being planted in the earth. I read some passages from the Scriptures and then follow the procedure as given in your minister's manual for committing a body to the ground. There is a committal for an unbeliever in the manual also. Conclude your part with prayer.

At this point several things might happen. If the deceased was in a masonic order, they may say a word or two and go through their ceremony.

Sometimes there is a military ceremony. Stand quietly and

simply observe the ritual with interest. If the military attache or the funeral director hands you the folded flag, go to the widow or to the designated family member and present the flag to that person. Say, "On behalf of the nation and for noble services rendered, I am honored to give this flag into your keeping as a symbol of our gratitude." Then you should step back.

After ceremonies at the grave are concluded, the funeral director usually has the pallbearers file by and lay their boutonnieres on the casket. Then the director will usually say, "This concludes our services." He might take that time to also make some general remarks.

Before the committal, ask him if he is going to conclude at the end of the ceremonies at the committal service. If he is not, then you should say, "On behalf of the family, I want to thank you for coming, for the floral tributes, and for all the expressions of love. This concludes our services. May God bless you."

Then you should immediately move to members of the family who are seated by the grave, extending your hand and heartfelt sympathies.

After you have greeted members of the family and others, you are free to go back to the hearse or to your car.

The funeral dinner is a wonderful opportunity for you to minister further to the family. Sometimes the family wants to invite everyone attending the funeral to the dinner. Usually the family will want you to announce this at the funeral or committal service. The appropriate time to announce the dinner would be after your final prayer at the funeral and before people view the body. If there is no committal service, your invitation should come during the closing remarks made by you or the funeral director.

Invariably the coordinator of the funeral dinner will ask you to get the family seated and have prayer. Call for attention, explain the directions about going through the buffet line (if applicable), whether beverages will be served, etc. Thank the women of the church for arranging the dinner and for preparing the food. Tell the people present to enjoy the fellowship and feel at home.

Request that the immediate members of the family be allowed to go through the line first. After instructions are given, pray over the food.

If possible you should stay for the dinner. After you have eaten, go to the members of the immediate family and bid them farewell. Assure them of your continued prayers.

On your way out of the building, stop by the kitchen and personally thank the coordinator and her helpers for their good work.

Chapter 15

The Role of A Minister's Wife

For almost 50 years I have had the privilege of observing two of the finest ministers wives in the world.

First, I observed my mother. Mother was a true co-pastor with my father--remaining in one church for over 30 years. My mother handled most of the administrative duties at the church, and she was also an outstanding preacher, teacher, and a recognized authority in Christian education.

While fulfilling these other duties, my mother also operated a successful Christian nursing home. Even though she was involved in all of this activity, she was a wonderful wife and mother.

The other minister's wife is my own wife. This remarkable lady has, for over 30 years, been a role model for many younger women. Her ability to change roles throughout the years has been remarkable.

We began our ministries together as music directors, then evangelists, then pastors, and now as directors of the U.S. Decade of Harvest. In all these roles she has been effective in her own ministries as a brilliant musician and effective conference speaker.

I believe her greatest effectiveness, however, has remained in the home where she has been a wonderful wife, mother, and grandmother.

The privilege of knowing these remarkable women over many years in a variety of settings has given me a perspective on the minister's wife which is somewhat unique. Using my mother and my wife as primary examples, and the observation of many other ministers' wives as supportive examples, I have tried to set down in writing for you what I believe to be the fundamental principles in the life of a successful minister's wife.

It is necessary from the very beginning to understand the complexity of the minister's wife. In many cases, the minister's wife has to deal with seven levels of relationships simultaneously.

1. *She is a unique person.*

No other person on earth is just like her. Few understand the significance of this statement. The minister must realize his wife can emulate other people in ministry, but she will forever be who she is as a unique human being. The minister would do well to appreciate and cultivate this uniqueness rather than try to deny the reality. Too many ministers have a preconceived idea of what a minister's wife should be and are afraid to allow their wives to be the delightful people the Lord intended them to become.

2. *She is uniquely a woman.*

It would seem, on the surface, this statement need not be made. However, it is vital to a good relationship and an effective ministry for the pastor to accept the reality of the difference God himself created between male and female. My counsel to young ministers is to simply have the will to understand.

Being a woman, the minister's wife has vastly different needs and functions from her husband. He needs to accept her different physical, psychological, spiritual, and sociological needs and functions as blessings, not as barriers to resist.

3. *She is a Christian woman.*

The moment she accepted Christ as Lord and Savior, she entered into an eternal relationship which would have its impact upon all of her earthly relationships, including her husband. She must maintain a personal relationship and loyalty to Christ which transcends all other alliances.

From time to time, even in a Christian marriage, her loyalty to God can come into conflict with obedience to her husband. A wife's obedience to her husband is a divine principle, but not at the cost of disobedience to a clear directive from her Lord.

4. *She is a Christian wife.*

She now faces all the responsibilities of marriage. Most women are extremely conscientious about fulfilling their roles as wives, but none so much as Christian wives. The minister needs to honor this in the woman he marries.

It is incumbent upon all husbands and especially Christian husbands to love their wives and encourage them. Too many ministers have been careless in making derogatory and thoughtless remarks in front of others concerning their wives. Because of her special relationship with God and her husband, she should be treated with respect.

5. *She is a minister's wife.*

This role adds another layer of responsibility upon a woman of God. Many ministers' wives feel inadequate to fulfill what they perceive as a very demanding task. The role of the minister's wife is not as difficult as it might first appear. The frustration comes from trying to meet the expectations of people.

The minister can be a tremendous help to his wife by being clear on his expectations and protecting his wife from unnecessary criticisms and unrealistic demands. He needs to take the lead in this area with a view of trying to ease the pressure on his wife, not add to it.

6. *She is a minister's wife, and she may be a mother.*

The pastor should realize the impact children will have upon his wife and ministry. The task of raising a family in a minister's home is formidable. Especially when the children are small, the physical demands on the mother are impossible for a man to completely understand.

My wife speaks of the times when our children were tiny as times of exhaustion. There were times, when the children were finally in bed, when she would go into the living room and just sit. She looked at nothing, she listened to nothing. She just sat there, relishing the moments of silence.

Both the pastor and the church need to be sensitive to these growing up years. Every effort should be made to lessen the responsibilities of the pastor's wife who has the primary task of raising a family in a ministerial setting.

7. *She may be a minister's wife and a mother who works outside the home.*

More and more of our ministers' wives are finding themselves in this almost inhuman situation. If a minister's wife has a choice in working outside the home, she would do well to think through the impact such a choice would have on her husband and family.

Most who work outside the home have no choice because of inadequate income from the ministry. In this circumstance, the church should not expect a minister's wife to have any regular responsibilities at the church.

To the contrary, the church should recognize that this woman is making it possible for their church to have a pastor and should seek to minister to her.

The husband, as busy as he might be, must take on his share of duties in the home while his wife struggles through this difficult period in her life and their ministry. It is imperative he arrange times of rest and relaxation for her.

In spite of the complexities inherent in the role of the minister's wife, there can be a sense of great fulfillment and resultant blessing in her efforts. I have chosen to list several principles I believe must be adhered to if the minister's wife is to be happy and effective in her God-given role.

Principle One

The effective minister's wife accepts her role. There was never any question by the ministers' wives in my family about their identity.

I have observed, through the years, that the most unhappy ministers' wives I have met have been those who have had a hard time coming to terms with the fact that when God called their husbands to ministry, He also called them.

It is a conflict in terms for a wife to say, "I am married to this man, but God called him to the ministry, not me." It would be like the president's wife saying, "The nation elected my husband, but it did not elect me as First Lady. Therefore, I will not accept my responsibilities as such."

The fulfilled and happy minister's wife is the one who is not seeking for her identity apart from her husband. She knows she has married in the will of God and accepts the role of the minister's wife as an ordained call of God to the ministry.

Principle Two

The effective minister's wife adjusts to her role. She finds the changes of location and assignments as challenges, giving her opportunities to minister and assist her husband in fulfilling his call.

I watched my wife in her first ministerial assignment as the wife of an associate minister. Because part of my job description was to serve as choir director, we were able to work closely together as a team in the area of music. Never once did she ask for financial remuneration for her work in the church. She delighted in being part of the whole church body. She sincerely sought to learn from the senior pastor's wife and became a close friend in spite of the disparity in age.

The Lord led us next into full-time evangelism. Never once did my wife complain about the change in ministry and the loss of a home base--a factor which is so very important to a woman. Instead, she threw herself into assisting my ministry in every way she could.

Her involvement in music was a great asset on the evangelistic field, but her greatest joy was working at the altars.

As a guest in many ministers' homes, she quickly adapted to helping the pastors' wives with kitchen duties whenever possible.

Following our time on the evangelistic field, my wife became a senior pastor's wife. Here again, she quickly adapted to the change, enjoying the various aspects of the ministry.

Because the children were small in our first pastorate, she had to carefully choose her weekly involvement in church ministry. Because of her musical ability, she chose to be an integral part of a growing music program.

At the same time she opened her home to many social events

and remained a constant source of encouragement to me as a young pastor.

In later years, my wife had to adapt to a life of travel and a national ministry based at the Assemblies of God headquarters. The demand for constant change and adapting to new surroundings and situations are weekly and at times daily occurrences. If my wife had chosen to resent any move or change of status in the ministry, she could have become unhappy and created great tension in our home.

Ministers' wives must be flexible and adaptable. The ministry to which she and her husband have been called is a living thing, subject to incredible variety and change.

Principle Three

The single greatest qualification to being a good minister's wife is simply being a good Christian. When you analyze the role of the minister's wife, about the only differences between that role and the role of a layperson are some counseling and ceremonial duties. All other qualifications to being an outstanding preacher's wife are the same as those necessary to be an outstanding Christian woman.

In 2 Corinthians 6, the apostle Paul is very concerned that the ministry is not blamed and used as an excuse for hardship. He begs us not to receive the grace of God in vain...*giving no offence in any thing, that the ministry be not blamed, but in all things approving ourselves as the ministers of God, in much patience, in afflictions, in necessities, in distresses.*

Many ministers' wives have fallen into the trap of blaming the ministry for forcing them to live a disciplined Christian life. They say "Well, I suppose I had better go to church tonight because I am expected to do so." No, she goes to church, is involved in the activities of the church as much as possible, and reaches out to people about her. She does not do these things because she is the wife of a minister, she does them because she is a dedicated Christian.

Some ministers and their wives blame the pressures of the ministry as the reasons for tension and unhappiness in their marriage. The ministry is no harder on a marriage than any other profession. In most cases, the ministry--which is much more than a profession--contributes to the joy and happiness of a marriage. If there is trouble in the home, the ministry should not be blamed. Attention should be turned to the people in the marriage.

The ministry does not cause neglect of wives and children, people do. The ministry does not cause tensions and trouble, people do. The ministry should never be blamed for a bad marriage.

Principle Four

Your children should not be examples to those they come into contact with simply because they are preacher's kids. They should be examples because they are Christians.

This is one principle which needs to be ingrained in every minister's home. The minister himself needs to be primarily responsible to practice this fundamental law in his household. However, I have observed minister's wives falling into the trap of saying to their children, "You know, people at the church expect you kids to be an example. What will the people think at the church if you don't go?"

Should minister's kids be faithful to church? Should they be involved in the activities of the church at their age level? Should they pray and read the Bible? **Absolutely! But they do not do these things just because they are PKs.** They do them for the same reason every other kid in the church should do these things.

More ministers' children have been destroyed because they have been made to go to church and make a show of religion for all the wrong reasons than because of any other factor. If they do things for people in the church, then, when they are gone from the home, the reasons for going to church and going through the motions of the Christian life will be gone.

From the day we began pastoring, we refused to let the people in our church hold our children up as examples. They were to be treated as individuals--just like every other child in the church. At home, they were encouraged and at times disciplined to be at church and involved in the things of God, not because they were preacher's kids, but because their parents wanted them to be disciplined followers of Christ.

Today our children are grown. They love the ministry, and they have fond memories of their growing up years. All of them are serving Jesus and active in the kingdom of God.

Many times I have been saddened as I listened to preachers' kids spewing out resentment toward their parents and the people in the church. At the heart of much of it was their resentment toward being forced to do things because they were put in the impossible position of being and doing what the people in the church expected, rather than serving the Lord. Don't allow this to happen to your children.

Principle Five

Prioritize and then calanderize. In other words, *seek first the kingdom of God and His righteousness, and let other things be add-ons.*

Allow me to attack a myth surrounding the life of the minister. The schedule of a pastor can be controlled at least 90 percent of the time. The pastor is not the victim or pawn of his people. He has every right to control his schedule.

Granted, there are men who do not choose to discipline their time or guide their people, but that is not the fault of the ministry.

In both the small and large churches I pastored, I discovered that emergencies and special events made up a very small percentage of my time. At least 90 percent, and sometimes even more of all church work is routine and subject to scheduling.

A minister's wife can help her husband immeasurably by getting out the calendar and sitting down with him to schedule priorities. *What day in the week is best for "family day?" What are the best times for meals? What time of the day is best for devotions? When should we take a break and go off ourselves? When can we plan for family vacations? What days will be devoted to family outings?*

Put these things on both your family calendar and on your pastoral calendar. These are your priorities. They are very important! Only critical illness, a death in the church, or very unusual circumstances should be allowed to interfere.

Some ministers have used the family as an excuse to be lazy or not get their church work done. There is always time for the great priorities of life. As a minister, your priorities are to achieve a balance between your family life and your church life.

Most pastors and wives who struggle with their schedules have not set schedules and lived by them. They are in the habit of reacting toward events rather than determining the quality of life. If you and your wife do not determine your own schedule, everyone else in your congregation will do so. The size of a congregation has nothing to do with this principle.

Very early in my ministry, God dealt with me about having my own sabbath and a day with my family. I set a day, then told my congregation about this day. I was amazed as the congregation broke out into applause when I gave the announcement and the reason behind it.

Very few of my days off were impacted by needs of the church during all of my 25 years of pastoral ministry. Of course, everyone, including my family, understood when a real emergency or crisis had to take priority over my day off. When those things happened, I tried to move my family day to another day that week.

Ministers' wives are responsible to respond to hurting people and to be part of the Lord's work as a helpmeet to her husband. However, she is not obligated to be the slave of the phone and everyone's whims.

A minister's wife must set her calendar as well. She must put the great priorities of life first. She must make time for God and for her family. What time is left, she should give it to the church.

She should encourage her husband, without nagging, to stick with a basic schedule. When we had a family night scheduled, we could say with integrity, "That night is already taken" when someone else wanted to fill it.

The bottom line to maintaining a schedule of priorities is desire. If you and your wife want to maintain a balanced life, you can do so most of the time.

Some time ago a pastor said to me, "I never seem to be able to get a day off, there is just too much to do . Did you ever take a day off?"

I replied, "Yes. Every week."

The pastor's mouth dropped open, and he then asked, "Even when you pastored a big church?"

"Even when I pastored a big church," I answered.

He then asked, "How in the world did you arrange that?"

I replied, "I arranged it because I wanted to!"

You see, we ultimately do what we want to do on a regular basis in spite of all the demands from others. We choose to serve God, have a family, build a church. We also determine the quality of those activities, under God.

Principle Six

Trust God and love your mate. A marriage is *built* on love, not trust. *Trust is earned*. Trust is *a by-product of a long-term relationship*. In the final analysis, God is the only person who can be absolutely trusted.

In no way am I advocating distrust, neither am I encouraging suspicion. However, too many ministers' wives are so afraid their husbands will think they do not trust them, that they allow conniving women and unhealthy practices to go unchallenged.

God has placed your wife in your life to be a helpmeet. It is wrong for your wife to be jealous and suspicious, but it is also wrong for her to allow your marriage and ministry to be threatened by outside circumstances. Your wife should be there to raise a red flag when necessary.

It's all right for her to give you a gentle warning about another woman she feels in her spirit is real trouble. It is all right for her to caution you about how to and how often you counsel certain women in your church.

Some of the greatest men in the church have fallen because no one had the courage to confront them about potentially dangerous relationships. No person is better equipped to do so than a loving wife who trusts her husband a great deal, but knows that "he who would not fall should not walk in slippery places."

This is a very difficult principle to communicate without sending the wrong message. Here again the key is balance. On the one hand your wife has to place a great deal of trust in you. She cannot protect you from every imagined pitfall and every morally corrupt person. Yet, on the other hand, you are human and subject to moral failure. You need a loving, responsible person in your life who loves you to death--a person who loves you enough to risk your displeasure in order to warn you of danger. Your wife is that person.

Principle Seven

Your wife should not seek a position in the church. She should let ministry flow toward her naturally. Too many ministers's wives are anxious to become such a "part of their husband's ministries," they force their will on others, and, in some extreme situations, remove others from places of authority in the church for all the wrong reasons.

As pastor, you could be placed in a very difficult situation if you were forced to satisfy the desires of your wife in the area of ministry in the church--especially if your wife is very aggressive. A minister's wife should never force her way to any kind of leadership. She can be an integral part of her husband's ministry without having an official position or department under her direction.

Let us assume there is a real need for leadership in the Women's Ministries of the church. Let us further assume the minister's wife is dynamic and the obvious person to lead Women's Ministries. It is not the role of the pastor or his wife to force the obvious. The decision to place the pastor's wife in charge of Women's Ministries should come from a non-pressured board or committee that makes these appointments.

A person's gifts will provide all the room needed for ministry. If the minister's wife is prayerfully patient, God will open doors no men can shut. The position might be the right one, but the timing might be all wrong. The minister's wife can be a great example of determining the will of God through openness to service and wisdom in decision making.

Principle Eight

A minister's wife must watch out for friendships that polarize. There are many ministers' wives who feel they need a close friend and confidante. Many times sincere ministers' wives have created and sustained a friendship based primarily upon personality and mutual interests, rather than spiritual need.

There is a vast difference between friendships in the church and confidantes in the church. Your wife should be friendly with everyone in the church. She can certainly have special friends in the church--based upon age, interest, and family--however, she needs to guard against becoming "buddy-buddy" with one or two women in the church.

For the younger minister's wife it is often safer to build a close friendship with a neighboring minister's wife.

Friendships in the church are safe only when they are open and inclusive. In other words, your wife's close friendship with someone in the church should not exclude others from being a part of her circle of love. One friend should never be allowed to cling to your wife and dominate her time and life. You should encourage her to guard against this.

A confidante is very dangerous in the local church. Almost without exception, what you say to anyone in your congregation should be said with the idea in mind that it will be repeated to others. Very few people are able to keep a confidence over the long haul. Your wife's conversations with church people should be such that what she says would not embarrass her if it were said from the pulpit.

In almost every situation, you wife's confidante should be a very spiritual, older, wiser woman. She should either be in the ministry, or she should be someone who has a long record of spiritual life and wise counsel. This person must also have a reputation for keeping confidences. Only in very rare situations can this person be in the church you pastor.

As I stated previously, in most cases it is wise for your wife to have as a confidante another minister's wife who lives close by.

Principle Nine

Your wife must choose to enjoy the ministry. I often say that happiness is between the ears. The happy and fulfilled ministers' wives I have observed have just as many excuses to be unhappy as anyone else. It is not so much what the ministry brings to your wife that counts. Rather, it is the attitude your wife brings to the ministry that becomes one of the great determining factors in her life.

She is a minister's wife. That is a fact. Short of some disaster or unforeseen change, she will be a minister's wife the rest of her life. It can be the most exciting, fulfilling, and rewarding life in the world, or, it can be the most demanding, frustrating, and unhappy life in the world. The difference is up to her.

After observing women in the ministry for close to 50 years, I believe that I can say--without fear of contradiction--that those who are called to the ministry have the greatest opportunity on earth. They not only make a positive impact on others, but they have the joy of knowing that all they do to the glory of God will someday meet with heaven's ultimate reward.

One day they will hear the Master say, "*Well done, thou good and faithful servant.*"